The true and not-so-true Story of the Airplane

WRITTEN & ILLUSTRATED BY

GIGI TEGGE

GREENE BARK PRESS PO BOX 1108 BRIDGEPORT, CT 06601

Publisher's Cataloging-in-Publication
(Provided by Quality Books, Inc.)

Wright vs. Wrong!

Printed in China. For information address Greene Bark Press,
PO Box 1108, Bridgeport, CT 06601

Library of Congress Cataloging in Publication Data
Tegge, Gigi
Wright vs. Wrong!: the true and not so true story of the airplane / written and illustrated by Gigi Tegge
p. cm.
Preassigned LCCN: 97-71282
ISBN: 1-880851-26-1
Summary: The Wright brothers solve some of the problems of flight which the Wrong brothers are unable to solve.
1. Aviation--History--Juvenile fiction. 2. Wright, Orville, 1867-1912--Juvenile fiction. 3. Wright, Wilber, 1871-1948--Juvenile fiction. 4. Kitty Hawk (NC)--Juvenile fiction. 5. Stories in rhyme. I. Title.
PZ7.T4444Wr1997 [E]
QB197-40401

To my Mom and Dad,
Don and Lucy Little

The brothers Wrong and the brothers Wright
Got together one fine night,
And they all wondered if they might
Invent an airplane to take flight!

If birds can fly, so can a man,
Thought brothers Wrong. They just began.
They flapped their arms. They jumped and ran.

But brothers Wright, they made a plan.
ORVILLE
WINGS
OPELLER
WILBUR

The brothers Wrong, they made plans, too.
They fed their minds on turnip stew.
They tried with boxes painted blue.

WRONG BROTHERS'
PLAN

1. Eat turnip stew.
2. Invent Airplane.
3. Take nap.

HOW DOES A BIRD FLY?
But brothers Wright, they knew what to do.
LUCY

The brothers Wrong said, "Me oh my!
A bicycle is what we'll try
To ride so fast through the sky."

WIRE
But brothers Wright, they bought supplies.
FABRIC
WIRE
LIST
WOOD
WIRE
FABRIC
FABRIC
WOOD

Next, the brothers Wrong attached springs
To other kinds of bouncy things.
They tied everything with purple strings.

But brothers Wright, they built some wings.

The brothers Wrong, they worked all night
With big balloons and a large white kite.
Yes, their airplane would be just right!

But brothers Wright said, "We'll get it right!"
GLIDER
WING – covered with fabric
WING
BRACING WIRE
WING STRUT
GLIDER-- will glide on air, using wings, like a bird.

Postmaster Tate
helped out.
And brothers Wright, they did not fret.
Their glider flew, as you can bet.
It flew as high as it could get!

But it was not an airplane quite yet.
GLIDER HAS TAIL ON BACK END
TAIL OR "RUDDER" IS FOR TURNING GLIDER.
GLIDER TAIL

The brothers Wrong, they began to fight.
One of their planes gave them quite a fright.
What, oh what, could make it right?

"An engine!" said the brothers Wright.

The brothers Wrong still tried to go.
They tied a crow to a big toe,
But still their airplane would not go.

The brothers Wright knew better, though.
PROPELLER
Engine makes propeller spin. When air pushes against the propeller, it makes the airplane "propel"-- or move forward by itself! Airplane has 2 propellers.

GLUEY GOO
The brothers Wrong knew what to do.
They caught eleven Meelee-moos
And stuck them on with gluey-goo.

But brothers Wright said, "That won't do."

Then brothers Wrong jumped up with glee
All they needed, don't you see,
Was a Zee-ba-womp and one small flea!
FLEA

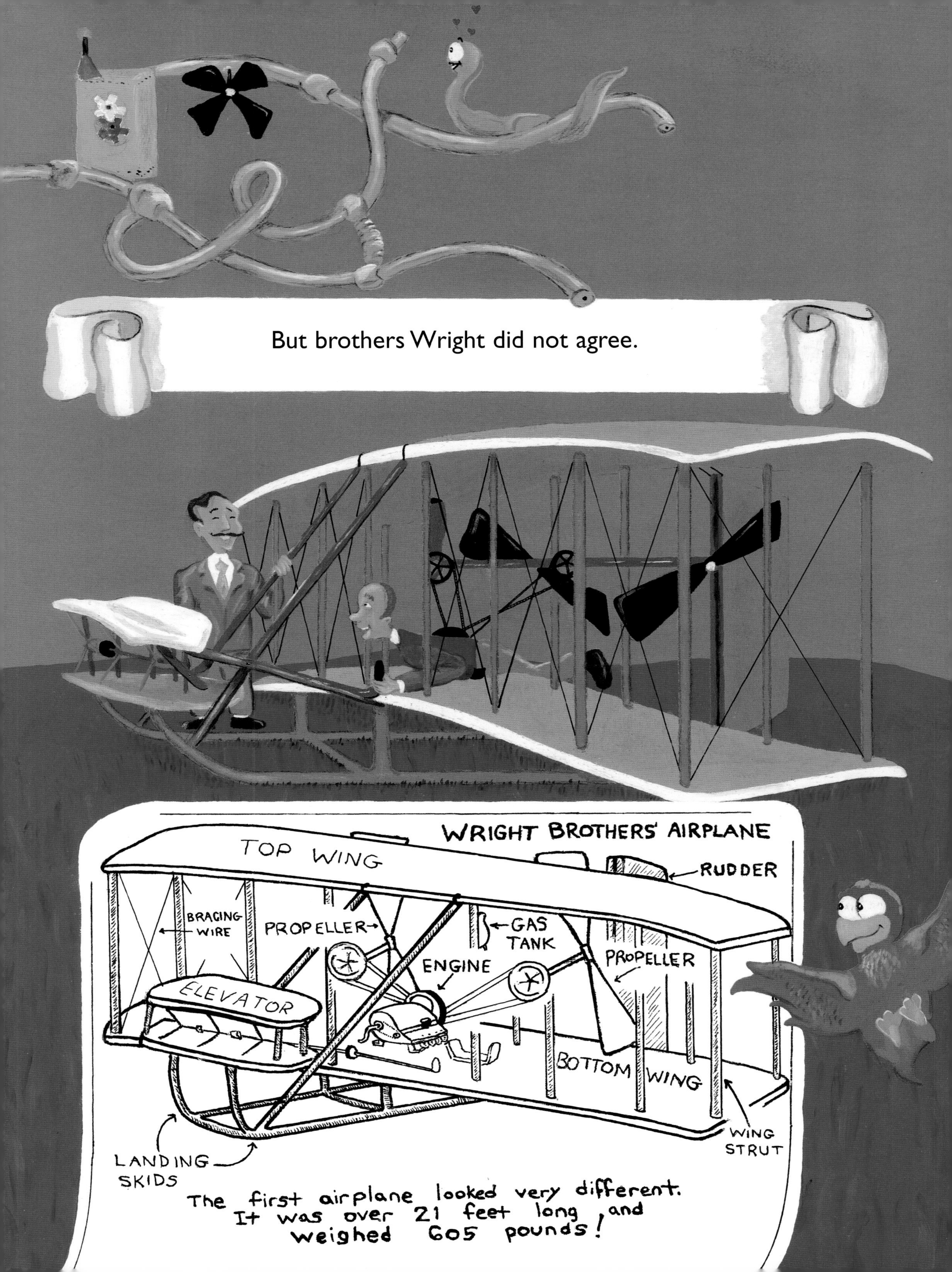
But brothers Wright did not agree.
WRIGHT BROTHERS' AIRPLANE
TOP WING
RUDDER
BRACING WIRE
PROPELLER
GAS TANK
ENGINE
PROPELLER
ELEVATOR
BOTTOM WING
WING STRUT
LANDING SKIDS
The first airplane looked very different. It was over 21 feet long and weighed 605 pounds!

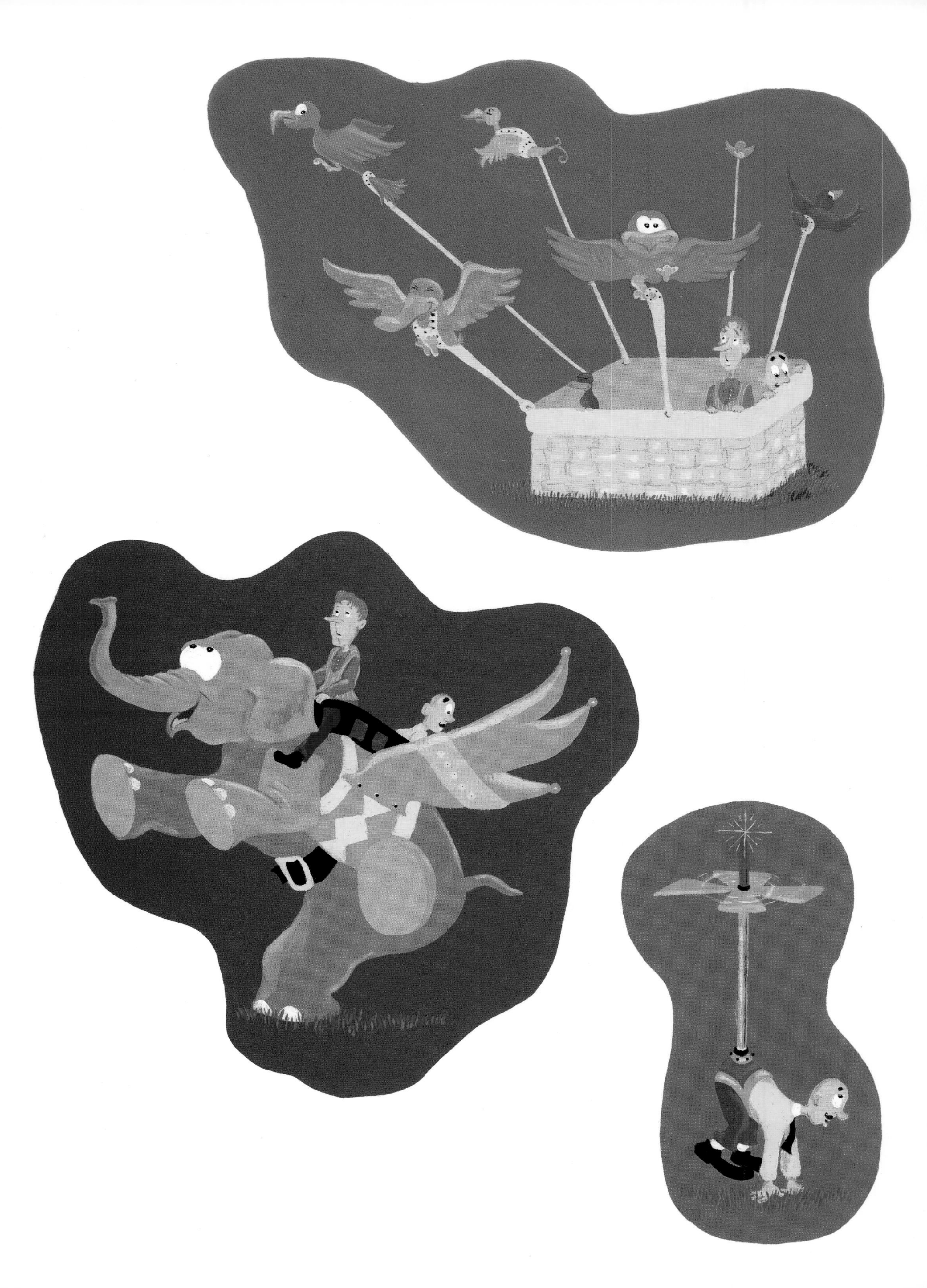

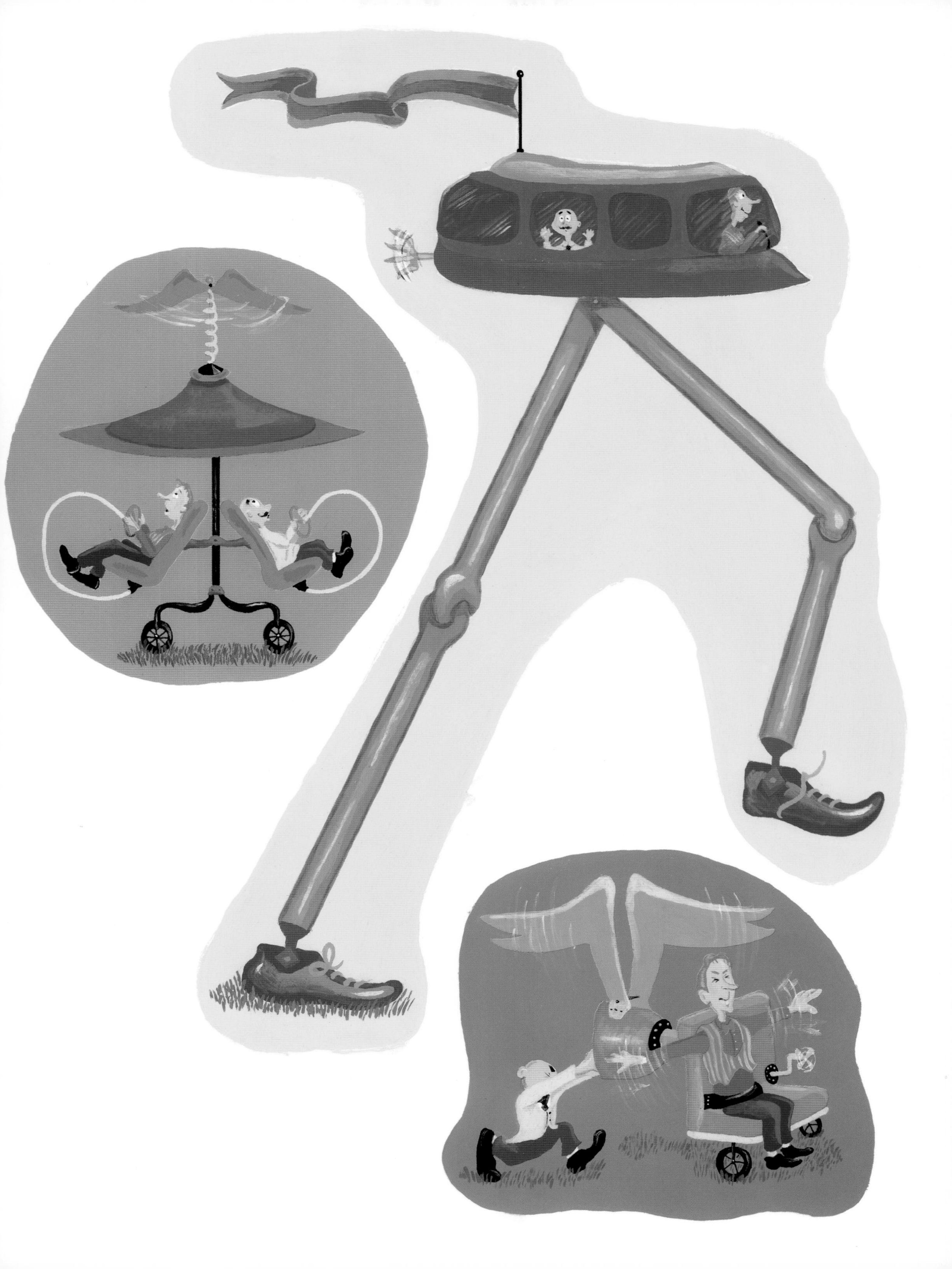

FLY
DON'T FLY

TRASH

Soon it finally happened! Orville Wright
Took off and flew with great delight.
What a day! What a sight!
That first amazing airplane flight!

So now we all know
That the brothers Wright were right!

This subconscious fear could account for much of the ridiculous pomposity which turns up in writing; its purpose is to screen out the real person.

SO MUCH FOR TALENT

It's time we mention the writing virus; there's a lot of it going around. I refer to an incurable disease called "talent."

A prevalent belief is that writing can be accomplished only by so-called *talented* persons. No one else need apply. Only a few gifted individuals are supposed to be able to perform this mysterious work of inscribing words on paper.

Garbage.

The French titan of literature, Gustave Flaubert, announced: "Talent is long patience."

To date, no one has located the seat of talent. Is it in the brain? The heart? The soul? Is it a muscle? Can it be operated upon when diseased? Can it be transplanted from husband to wife?

Does it even exist as a separate entity? If it is so mysterious, why even bother about it?

More important by far to a would-be writer is a highly unmysterious quality known as *self-discipline.*

Teachers of writing soon discover that "talented" persons are common. Much less common are those "talented" persons who are willing to put in the long hours of hard work required to develop their skills, who have the fortitude to endure the frustrations and failures which inevitably occur when they try to hone "talent" into something more useful.

I know persons without a trace of what is commonly called "talent" who have written books which have been bought and paid for by publishers. Apparently it didn't occur to these deprived individuals that they lacked "talent;" they merely turned on their energy and persistence.

One of the worst traps for a young writer is baited with the gushing praise of a friend or relative who carols:

"Gollee! You're really *talented,* you know?"

Whereupon Young Writer sits back and preens while some no-talent, mule-headed opportunist grinds out the words and gets the book published.

Remember who won the Hare & Tortoise Grand Prix?

DEAR SIR, YOU CUR

Some of the best writing I read is in the letters-to-the-editor column of newspapers. Most of the authors, I suppose, don't even think about talent; they merely want to get something off their chests.

I have a friend, a former country storekeeper in my rural neighborhood, who had this habit. I don't recall that he ever boasted about his writing "talent." I do remember that, like most red-blooded Americans, he hated the telephone company and spent a surprising amount of his time trying to give indigestion to Mother Bell. (This, of course, was only when he wasn't occupied in shaking up the power company.) Once, in high (but humorous) dudgeon, he wrote this letter to the editor:

> "Dear sir,
>
> "Some years back there was a play called 'Cheaper By The Dozen' based on the theory that if you bought in quantity you could make enormous savings.
>
> "I recently discovered that the digit-happy phone company accepted this principle.
>
> "We live some ten miles from town and our phone service is referred to as 'suburban service.' This means that for $3.75 per month you shared a line with seven others and if you even wanted the time of day it would be better to call in after midnight . . .
>
> "I was offered better service for a price. The price is computed on a mileage basis . . .
>
> "However since our community is sparsely settled we are rated at something around $2.00 per mile per month for a private line. To get any service I could use I have been

paying $18.25 per month plus tax . . .

"Recently the company put on a spring planting project and buried their cables. With the improvement they decided to improve their service and give all their 8-party lines 4-party service at the same $3.75 per month.

"I therefore decided that I would be ahead to have 4 phones on one line for $15.00 than one phone at $18.25. I had three more phones installed and I am especially proud of the new underwater phone that was installed in the bathroom. You see I like to sing in the shower and with this new hydrophone I am able to share my golden baritone with others. In fact I am receiving so many requests for some of my better renditions such as 'The Road to Mandalay' and 'Asleep in the Deep' that I am considering putting them on tape.

"So now I have a phone in every room, all on one private line at a saving of $3.25 per month and when I receive a call our home sounds like the little Bavarian clock shop at high noon."

Isn't that lovely? Even a non-professional can occasionally set gongs vibrating in the inner offices of the telephone company.

THE WRITER AS A BLEEDER

Almost everyone likes to read a breezy, humorous bit of writing. One gets the impression from words like these that they tripped lightly out of the author's mind in little more time than it takes to read them.

Not so, unfortunately. Writers of this dancing prose often complain that getting the light effect is a slow process consisting mostly of painful revision. The creation of written humor seems to be a highly unhumorous undertaking.

Some writers of other kinds of material, though, do seem to grind out millions of words without apparent pain. The creator of Perry Mason, Erle Stanley Gardner, dictated his many novels into a recorder rapidly enough to keep three secretaries busy transcribing.

But the writer type known as the "bleeder" is probably much more common. This person writes slowly and painfully, grimly squeezing each word from a reluctant brain. The great American novelist, Thomas Wolfe, once remarked: "Writing is easy. Just put a sheet of paper in the typewriter and start bleeding."

The bleeder may be satisfied if he turns out half a page of acceptable manuscript during a day's work; a speeder may feel guilty if he doesn't finish 20 pages. But a first draft is only part of the job. The speeder may have to revise heavily; the bleeder may have to do little or none.

Writing is thinking on paper but that's only Phase I. Phase II is a transfer process; the information on the paper must register in the mind of a reader. Most writing, like that in a daily newspaper, never gets beyond Phase II.

The best writing advances to Phase III—emotion. This polished product succeeds not because of its informational content but because it transmits *feeling.* It causes readers to laugh or cry or curse.

A reader wants to respond emotionally. Feeling is an important girder in the bridge the writer must build between his own mind and that of the reader. If a writer fails to stir emotion, he is likely to bore his reader and then even the information load is likely to sink out of sight.

A reader demands to be *stirred,* not just informed.

THINGS ARE TOUGH ALL OVER

Be kind to your writing teachers; they lead a hard life.

If, as a student of writing, you sometimes feel like a duck in quicksand, save a tear for your teacher, who may be saddled with an impossible job.

A teacher can take a student of writing a short distance along this bumpy road but inevitably comes a screeching halt. A teacher can teach mechanics; a teacher can often demonstrate how a sentence written one way is more effective than a sentence written another way (without always being able to say exactly *why);* a teacher can say: "You lost my interest on page two."

But judgments like this are always subjective; a good writing teacher, unlike a good teacher of mathematics, can never say: "This is absolutely right and this is absolutely wrong." In writing, one man's meat is another man's indigestion. Good teachers understand this basic truth and it is important that students learn not to expect good teachers to make neat, flat, right-wrong judgments about writing.

It's time to go bicycle riding. Remember when you learned that fundamental human skill? If you couldn't figure it out for yourself, your instructor told you where to sit (this is the easy part), where to put your feet and hands, how to operate the brakes (we hope) and how to get on and off without smashing your head. Then your instructor walked alongside and balanced the flopping monster while you waddled your white-knuckled way toward disaster.

Inevitably there came that breath-catching instant when your instructor let go, usually saying something cheerful like "It's your bicycle . . . ride it!" and then quickly stepping behind a tree.

Then, in your moment of truth, you had to do it yourself, because to this day no one has come up with a workable rule for balancing a bicycle.

Inevitably, there must come the instant when your writing teacher says: "It's your mind. I know you can write with it. So write!"

In his moment of truth, a writer must do it himself, because to this day no one has come up with a workable rule for inscribing words on paper.

Sustained by his private strengths, threatened by his private weaknesses, the rider and the writer stagger down the road together.

From behind the tree, the instructor can only wave . . . and hope.

Moral: Be kind to your writing teachers; you may have no other witnesses to the accident.

BOUNCE A BALL AGAINST CARNEGIE HALL

The musician who hears the thunderous applause of a sophisticated audience is obviously enjoying himself hugely. But was he enjoying himself during those thousands of hours of tedious practice which preceded his appearance at Carnegie Hall?

How many times does a tennis champion have to slap a ball against a wall before his magic moment of triumph?

So it is with writing. Even more so, perhaps, with writing.

Now and then someone asks: "Do you enjoy writing?"

In a fit of honesty, I answer: "I enjoy the money I make from writing. Sometimes I enjoy reading my writing. I enjoy getting compliments on my writing. I enjoy knowing that having my writing published makes me just a little bit more than a face in the crowd. But do I enjoy the actual act of writing? No; most of the time, I don't. I enjoy *having written;* I enjoy that immensely, but that's another thing."

A newspaper reporter was sent to interview an old, old man on the occasion of the oldster's 100th birthday. After hard thought, the reporter asked: "Sir, if you were to condense your 100 years of life and experience and suffering and achievement into one sentence, what would that sentence be?"

The old man pondered, then lifted his head and rasped: *"There is no such thing as a free lunch."*

THE COTTON-PICKIN' CORN PICKER

All of the fine newspaper writing isn't in *The New York Times*. Some of it is in the *Skagit Valley Herald*.

The *Skagit Valley Herald* is published in Mount Vernon, Washington, in case you haven't heard of it, and I suspect that Mount Vernon (and perhaps the whole Skagit Valley) is one of the world's more interesting places. I offer in evidence the following piece of stunning writing by a certain Mary Vlahovich:

"That cotton-pickin' corn picker on the John Byrd place on Cape Horn Road burned and burned. It started at 1 p.m. and was finally out at 6:30 p.m. and 17 firemen were involved before the smoke finally disappeared.

"Like I said, the fire started in the field at 1 p.m. Friday. They called Whitey Mefford who operates the Grandy Creek Grocery and is a member of the Birdsview Fire Department. He used a dry chemical extinguisher from the store to put out the blaze.

"The corn picker is owned by the Pacific Fruit Co. of Burlington. The tractor pulling it was a John Deere 700. After the fire, the rig was left sitting in the field to cool off and at quitting time a driver, I don't know his name, hooked the tractor and the corn picker on the back of a pickup truck and headed for the shop in Burlington.

"He went west on Cape Horn Road to Lusk Road and turned toward the highway. It was then he noticed in his rear-view mirror the tractor was flaming again.

"Folks at the Midway Valley Grocery saw the flaming apparatus go by and called the Birdsview Fire Department. In the meantime, one Birdsview volunteer fireman, Dick Coesens, had seen the burning procession and was following. When the parade got to Grandy Creek Grocery, Mefford got in line and the procession turned down Russell Road toward the fire department.

"Everything was under control, it seemed, but in front of the Dan Dellinger place the drag line on the tractor broke and punched a hole in the tractor's fuel tank, which didn't exactly help any. About 200 feet farther, in front of the Gus Gerret place, the fire truck met the procession so everybody stopped and put the blaze out with dry chemicals and lots of water and when the fire was out they decided to clear the road. The whole procession started up again and went the 300 yards to the fire hall.

"The job of putting fire equipment away was under way at 5:45 p.m, when smoke from the tractor was again discovered. They soaked it down again and so, at 6 p.m., the driver with toasted farm equipment started back toward the highway.

"He got to the Vern Davis place about 300 yards north on Russell Road when he saw smoke pouring from the tractor differential, so nothing to do but turn around and head back to the fire hall. Three firemen were still there and they soaked it down good.

"Altogether about $800 damage was done. The cause was determined to be oil mixed with corn tassles which had ignited the exhaust system. Finally about 6:30 the fire was finally out and everybody went home. The corn picker spent the night in the fire hall yard, just to be handy.

"There were 17 men who answered all the various alarms. They were all of the Birdsview Fire Department, according to Sam Jones, fire department secretary. Among the last five who handled hoses were Ralph, Tom and Sam Jones, Glen Bust and Gus Gerrit.

"The guy who missed the whole thing was Chief Ken Hollinback. He was away."

I ask you: Could anyone, anywhere, have written that story better? By itself, it's a journalism textbook.

WORD PLAY

You'll be pleased to hear that even writing teachers have their problems when they turn to writing. Here is a sentence from a college teacher's book about writing:

"Effective expression involves appropriateness for the significance of what it is we have to say."

Anyone who can tell me what that means, in 1000 words or less, will win the grand prize: a lifetime supply of used typewriter ribbons.

SOMETHING TO THINK ABOUT

There's a lot of talk in schools these days about failure and how it's a bad thing. Sure; we'd all rather succeed all the time.

Most professional writers know about failure. Some of them think they invented it. Overcoming "failure" is almost a way of life for a professional writer. Of course, everyone's life is spotted with a certain amount of failure; it's a common tax deduction.

Failure, according to popular definition, consists of an attempt to do something which does not succeed immediately.

To that, I say "HUMBUG!"

That isn't failure, that's *education.* The best education tool in this world is called failure by those who have never thought hard about it. The reason "failure" is such a good education tool is that it burns itself into your mind: you REMEMBER it. And if you don't, your friends remind you, right?

Failure exists, but failure is not what happens when you try and don't succeed. Failure, in its pure form, is what happens when you die without having *tried* anything.

And the subject of next week's sermon will be: "Be kind to cockroaches; they may inherit the world."

SOMETHING MORE TO THINK ABOUT

"You write with ease to show your breeding, but easy writing makes demmed hard reading."
—Richard Brinsley Sheridan

"The writing habit of mind is not the same as the talking habit of mind. Writers have stories they'll never write because they've talked them too often. The stories got into a cocktail party talk-track and never got out. If talked onto tape and then transcribed they might still be wrenched into print, but as of now they have never been on paper. There is a common illusion among would-be writers that merely thinking or telling stories and wanting to write them makes them actual writers. It doesn't. Only a writer who writes is a writer."

—George Riemer

3. Don't Just Sit There; Write

The first word appears on paper, struggles for survival, then is joined by a second. Then comes the population explosion—numbers Three and Four.

The writing job has begun; for the writer, the battle is half won. Getting started is that important. Any trick a writer can play on his balky mind, no matter how sneaky, is legitimate. All is fair in love, war and getting started writing.

The seed from which any piece of writing grows is a basic idea. The four-year-old who looks out the window at a wet, cold world and wails, "Ma, whut kin I do now?" is the blood relative of the teenager who curls his lip at his English teacher and mutters: "I ain't got nuthin' to write about."

That's dumb. The *very idea.* The world is chuck-full to slopping-over with things to write about. Everybody is an expert in something. Maybe your something is Bowie knives or toy trains or Edsels or leaky boats; whatever it is, you know a few facts about it that not everybody knows. So write them down; share your wisdom with the world. The world may not love you for it but it may notice you, at least.

Being noticed is important and writing can do this for a person.

Clue One: It's easier to write about something you care about than something you don't give a whoop about. You might fool yourself about this but you will never fool a reader.

Clue Two: Somewhere in the world there is somebody who wants to read about what you want to write about. Maybe several somebodies. Maybe even your English teacher. So write it down and turn it in and let the chips fall. You have nothing to lose but your hangups.

The most common question asked of a professional writer is: "Where do you get your ideas?"

Apparently the would-be writer has a serious problem in this area. When I am asked that question, I usually reply: "How does one *keep* from getting ideas?"

If idea production were the heaviest cross borne by a professional writer, the literary life would be simple. Usually, the professional has many more ideas for pieces of writing than he has hours in which to write.

However, it may not have been that easy in the beginning. Somewhere along the way, he has discovered that ideas clutter the air like smog and all he needs to do is train his mind to act like a filter. It is simply a matter of being in the right place with the right receptacle.

The trouble with smog particles, though, is that they go as they came, fluttering on the breeze. A writer cannot depend on his mind to produce the kind of idea he needs at the precise moment he needs it. So he makes a habit of trapping ideas on tape or on file cards or in a file folder. To a professional writer, an idea file is as important as life insurance. In fact, it *is* insurance for a long, productive writing life.

Students would be well advised to start the same kind of file before the moment of need, as the smiling morticians say on television.

My personal preference is for the file folder system. Then, when I stumble across information relating to a particular idea, I clip it or write a note and pop it into the folder. If years pass between starting of the file and using it, I may find that much of my research has already been done, almost without my knowing it.

FAUCETS, HOT AND COLD

The second most popular question asked of professional writers is: "Do you work regular hours?"

I can't explain why this should seem so important to would-be writers. Personally, I wish they would stop asking the question because I've never found it easy to answer. I favor the Flannery O'Connor reply: "No, I don't work regular hours but I sit at the typewriter for regular hours." I agree with O'Connor that if one places oneself often enough in a position where writing can happen, some writing will happen. If you need a rule to cling to, there's a good one.

By this time, I hope, you have been disabused of the notion that a professional writer can sit down to his writing machine, turn the faucet and spew words. For one thing, the mind is like a muscle; it needs to be warmed up before it can work efficiently. Some writers warm up for the day's work by writing a personal letter or two. (A word of warning: When I use this method, I usually wind up the day with a great output of letters and nothing else. I'd rather write letters than books, I guess.)

A cold brain can be stirred into activity by writing gibberish. Simply type or scribble the first words to come into your head, not caring if they make sense, assuming that you will throw them away. Even a senseless scrawl can serve a purpose. If it does nothing else, this kind of scribbling may help to teach you that all your prose is not deathless, that in a wastebasket, there is always room for one more.

It is better to write badly than not to write at all. Sometimes very bad writing can be saved by revision; sometimes writing that looked very bad yesterday looks much better today and better yet tomorrow.

It's worth repeating: Half the battle is won when the first word is written. You wouldn't believe the wild contortions professional writers go through to avoid writing that first word of the day. Pencils must be sharpened; typewriters cleaned and ribbons changed; filing demands to be done; the cat must be let out; that filthy window must be cleaned; shelves of books must be rearranged; a letter must be mailed; the cat must be let back in.

All of these things cry out to be accomplished before the writer dares to sit down to his day's labor. A truly dedicated writing-avoider can usually come up with enough busy work to keep himself from writing well into the afternoon and really, is there any point in even starting so late in the day?

An actress who turned writer in her declining years said that when she found that she didn't want to start writing, her best excuse was to defrost the refrigerator. (Around our house, when I cleverly put off writing, the process is now known as defrosting the refrigerator.) This is an ingenious stratagem, because defrosting a refrigerator can use up an enormous amount of time and cause a fantastic clutter, but it has serious limitations. After all, how many times can one defrost a refrigerator during a single week? And even if one got a routine established of, say, three times a week, the silly machine would probably get sick from all that defrosting and the replacement would defrost itself automatically.

So if you have trouble getting started writing, you are normal. The professional has learned to accept this aspect of his life as merely one more thing he gets to whine about. He knows that if he sits down to write and nothing happens, this is not an excuse for charging off to play golf. He sits some more . . . and some more, knowing that if he gives his mind the opportunity to write often enough and long enough, it will.

Then he charges off to play golf.

WRITE, DON'T BLAB

A writer I know who turns out huge amounts of high quality wordage once commented that an experience didn't seem complete to him until he'd told someone about it. Right there, of course, is the secret of his great writing drive. This compulsion "to tell someone" may be the trait which divides writers from non-writers.

The basic urge, of course, is a common one but the person who puts it on paper is not like the person who spews it into a telephone mouthpiece. I know persons who claim to be writers who are only talkers; the difference is important.

There will be times when a student must decide whether he wants to write an experience . . . or talk it. Many professional writers resolutely refuse to tell a story until they have first transcribed it to paper. Smart, smart . . .

A student pregnant with an idea for a composition might be wise to keep his baby secret until it can be given a proper sendoff—on paper.

Some bigdomes have discovered that the most prized reward of marriage is not what you might think; it's *companionship.* That breaks down like this: someone to tell your troubles and triumphs to. In a good marriage, it works both ways.

A wife or husband is someone whose ears are available for the relating of experiences—as my writer friend would say, for the *completing* of experiences by telling someone about them. Partners in silent marriages are missing at least half the fun. It seems likely that these are the persons who sit in taverns and country clubs, completing an experience by telling it to the person on the next stool.

Writers have a big advantage over ordinary folk; they can complete an experience by putting it on paper. If their words are published, they can complete the experience hundreds of thousands of times, by telling hundreds of thousands of people.

Writing, they say, is lonely work. This is true, in a way; it is work not usually done in a crowded auditorium. In another way, though, a writer is the least lonely of human beings because through the marks he makes on paper, he can cast lines out to anyone in the world who can read. At last count, there were quite a few of those.

Listen to me, students: This peculiar push you feel, this creative instinct, this urge to bring forth this baby that is so distinctly yours, is a very special thing, a very delicate thing. Respect it; guard it carefully. Save all your creative energy for the moment when you face the blank sheet of paper.

Tell your story once—and tell it on paper.

THE BLUE FLASH AND OTHER NONSENSE

Time to put another dead horse into its final resting place, six feet under. The horse was called "Inspiration."

No professional writer facing deadlines, who must turn

out words or starve, dares to wait for that lame nag "Inspiration" to plod across the finish line.

Inspiration? It is said that Joseph Conrad sometimes would cry because he dreaded going in and settling down to the writing task. But he did it, inspiration or no.

The impression among non-writers is that writing is performed in a kind of creative frenzy, a glassy-eyed trance in which words gush forth. Not so.

My writing place has a spectacular view of southern Oregon and northern California—forests, mountains and long reaches of blue-gray sky, all of which is visible through large windows. Now and then someone sees my writing place and exclaims: "Ah! I see where you get your Inspiration!"

Big deal. When I'm writing, I'm not looking at the view. I am not even dimly conscious of the view; I am creating my own view in my brain and hoping that it is being transcribed to the paper in my typewriter. A writer who is writing is concentrating so intensely that he is only faintly aware of what goes on around him.

Instead of a hilltop office, I could have one in a basement. I would probably accomplish just as much in the basement. I'm glad my writing room is on a hilltop, though, because I think I go more often to this pleasant place with the sweeping view than I would go to a basement. Another trick . . .

I know a writer who has an office downtown in a busy, smoggy city. Almost every day he goes there to write. He writes more than I do and he writes better than I do. If you can explain this, I wish you wouldn't.

It's important, I think, for a professional or a student to have a private, personal place in which to write. This matters, because once the refrigerator is defrosted and you have begun the writing process, it is important that it not be interrupted. Once your brain has developed momentum, it must be asked to produce all the words it has in stock at the moment.

Distractions and interruptions are a writer's deadly enemies. Snarl at them; it helps.

In a moment of desperation, when your brain seems locked up tight, it may help to change your writing method. If you normally write by hand, try typing. If you normally type, try writing by hand. If both of these methods fail, try talking into a tape recorder, then transcribe later. There is more than one way to stimulate a cold, lazy brain.

The great American novelist, Sinclair Lewis, once remarked that he divorced his first wife because she could never understand that he was doing something very important when he seemed to be merely looking out the window.

Let's lay to rest once and for all this notion that a writer is a person who operates in a creative frenzy. The typical successful writer is notable not for the wild light in his eyes but for his self-discipline. In other words, he is able to concentrate time and energy on the job at hand.

If doing the job means that he must neglect his social life, his relatives and even his dog, he does so. If much writing is to be done, writing must come first.

Students may feel that they needn't be so single-minded as a professional since writing, for a student, is just a small part of a busy life. But this argument can be turned around: Simply because there are so many other demands on students' time, they must be even more disciplined than the professional.

CLOCK WATCHING FOR FUN AND PROFIT

I am often asked if I put in an eight-hour day at writing. I am petrified by the thought. My feeling is that about 10 consecutive eight-hour days of writing would put me in the hospital suffering from terminal fatigue. Some writers, I am told, are able to put in long, hard days for months at a time without ill effects; I think these individuals are being terribly unfair.

For most of the professionals I know, a four-hour daily stint is considered sufficient. Once in a while, under deadline pressure, they will have to work far into the night but this kind of punishment is avoided as much as possible. Much more important than the length of the work period is its regularity. Only regular writing can make writing a habit.

Sometimes it helps when beginning the writing struggle to think of a piece of writing not as a single entity, but as a collection of related parts. Research often is one part and outlining another. Every piece of writing has a beginning and a middle and an end. It isn't necessary—and sometimes not desirable—to wrestle with all the elements at once. Separate the job into segments, concentrate on a chosen segment, then move on to the next. In other words, cut the writing job down to a size your brain can handle at a given moment.

The opening of a piece of writing is enormously important (we'll talk more about that later), but you don't necessarily have to start work at that point. You can start in the middle and work toward both ends. Or, if a socko ending pops into your head, get it on paper before it slips away, then work back from there.

One shouldn't be alarmed when writing a first draft threatens to become a rather disorderly process. Time enough later to bring order out of chaos. It may well develop that if you flutter around a bit in turning out a first draft, your writing will be less stiff than if you had marched grimly from Point A to Point B to Point C.

HELP FROM THE BACK OF THE BRAIN

You have a writing problem you can't solve? You have everything but a punchy ending for your composition?

You've struggled and squirmed and bled but nothing comes? You feel the idea is there somewhere in the nooks and crannies of your mind but it won't come out and show its face?

To professional writers, this happens all the time. Most writing is done with the conscious mind but the subconscious is a strong ally. Unfortunately, it's an independent ally. It will work for you but only in its own good time.

It is fairly common for a professional, faced with an apparently insoluble writing problem, to worry it around in his mind while staring at the bedroom ceiling, then go to sleep. Upon awakening, he discovers with delight that the problem has been solved, without any apparent effort on his part. To many psychologists, the explanation is simple: The writer's subconscious has been at work.

It would be a mistake to assume that the subconscious mind is going to solve all one's writing problems but one would be just as foolish to ignore it. To make use of the subconscious, one must first stir the problem around in the conscious mind; this seems to be very important. Then one should deliberately put the problem aside and sleep, or be otherwise distracted for an extended period.

Try this trick the next time your conscious mind lets you down. If it doesn't work, try it again. If it still doesn't work, admit the truth: You've got a dumb subconscious.

You've allowed me to yammer a lot about the importance of getting those first few words down on paper, and you're impressed, aren't you?

Well, once started writing, I'm sorry to say, you can't afford to relax, for there's another little troll under the bridge.

Once started, you may need some help to avoid stalling. Let's say that your idea has jelled and you have leaped the first hurdle; the words are appearing on paper. At this moment, remember: This is *first draft* and it's not being engraved in stone. Don't be too finicky at this point. The too-finicky writer is the one who winds up staring a hole in the wall as his momentum slips out the window and his once-warm idea slides into the refrigerated section of his mind, whereupon the door slams shut and the light goes out. (You know how it is with refrigerators.)

The trick is to keep the words flowing, rolling, sliding onto the paper. You're *creating* at this stage, not being picky-picky. Go with the flow, then push it a little, just sort of nudge it along. Before your eyes, a few words turn into a sentence, a sentence into a paragraph and a paragraph into a composition . . . in the rough.

Oh, sure, some jagged edges need knocking off, a couple of those sentences are miserable examples of human English and there's kind of a sag there in the midsection but what the heck . . . it's not supposed to be a polished masterpiece at this stage. At least the skeleton is there and most of the muscles, too, and even a decent amount of skin. The job isn't finished but it's more than started, much more. What is needed now is some patient revision, always remembering that Frankenstein's monster wasn't built in a day.

Put the words away for a few hours or a few days, whatever you can afford. Looked at later, words have a way of seeming better than before, or worse, but always different. Cut away at the fat, add muscle, lay on a beauty mark here and there, cut away a little more fat, add that explosive ending that just popped into your head out of nowhere . . .

Well, howdydo, Mr. Monster! You're really quite handsome!

SOMERSET WAS TRICKY. TOO

The famous fiction writer, Somerset Maugham, once advised a young writer: "Always stop work for the day leaving the last sentence unfinished. When you look back the next day at what you've written, it's too awful to go on with, but you start by finishing that sentence."

The best thing about that idea is that it works. Try it sometime.

SEND YOURSELF A CARE PACKAGE

If you care about what you are writing, if you really care in your heart and soul and mind, you are certain to write better than if you don't care.

If you care, you have strong feelings to transmit to paper. Really good writers can fake emotion, and make the reader feel emotion, but it's always better if writers feel it themselves.

What follows is an example of emotional writing, attributed to Eddie Benton of the American Indian Movement:

INDIANS' PRAYER OF THANKSGIVING

"Oh, dear Lord, we thank you from the depth of our hearts and the wellspring of our souls. We beseech Thee to accept our humble words of gratitude for all that you have done for Indian people.

"Dear Lord, we thank you for poverty, starvation, infant deaths, a 44-year life span, diseases like smallpox, diphtheria, tuberculosis and V.D. We thank you for alcoholism and suicide.

"We thank you for slum landlords and outhouses. Dear Lord, we thank you for unemployment, relief rolls and food stamps. We thank you for missionaries, their hollow words and used clothing, old basketballs, mismatched shoes and evening gowns.

"We thank you for B.I.A. and all land grabbers. We thank you also for crooked politicians, hard-hearted university officials and money-hungry traders. We thank you for the fourth-rate education perpetuated by the B.I.A. and the Churches. We thank you for pollution that fills our streams and kills our fish and game.

"We thank you for 389 broken treaties. We thank you for Sand Creek, Wounded Knee and the Trail of Tears, as well as all scalp hunters. We thank you for extermination,

termination and assimilation of a proud, noble race. And bless all those anthropologists who dig up our dead. We thank you for loyal sympathetic understanding police, riot helmets, Mace, billy clubs and dogs.

"And, Lord bless all the apples, sellouts, and Uncle Tomahawks, for they walk with race haters, bigots, and desecrators.

"Bless all that are blind to Peace, Brotherhood and Indian unity.

"And we especially want to thank the churches for their spirited, well-organized fund raising drives using Indian people and their conditions as incentives for appeals.

"Lord, we thank you for suffering and heartaches that are caused by hate, greed. Bless America—Home of Freedom and Justice for all?"

When you care, you write more effectively than when you are just going through the motions. Try to write about what you care about. Your readers will notice.

SOMETHING TO THINK ABOUT

Abu-R-Rahman III, a Moor, ruled Spain as caliph and lived it up as only a Moorish ruler could. Somehow he found time to write the following:

> "I have now reigned 50 years, in victory or peace, beloved by my subjects, dreaded by my enemies, and respected by my allies. Riches and honors, power and pleasure, have waited on my call, nor does any earthly blessing appear to have been wanting to my felicity. In this situation I have diligently numbered the days of pure and genuine happiness which have fallen to my lot; they amount to 14."

WORD PLAY

From a business magazine: "Marvin J. Veltkamp has joined Zondervan Publishing House as controller. He was formerly with Keebler Biscuit Co., Schulze-Burch Biscuit Co., and Waste Management, Inc."

I can't say exactly why, but for some reason, I think that collection of words is hilarious and I don't even know Marvin J. Veltkamp. Is there something wrong with me?

"A combed writing will cost both sweat and the rubbing of the brain. And combed I wish it, not frizzled or curled."

—Owen Fellthan, 1628

4. The Mechanical Jungle

Let's all groan together, and grumble a bit, too, because we're going to talk for a while about the unromantic side of writing.

Writing can be split down the middle into two main chunks, one stamped "Creative" and the other "Mechanical," but separating writing in this way is no easier than slicing a stringy, gristly cut of beef with a dull knife.

The mechanical side of writing involves mundane matters like (if you'll pardon the expressions) spelling, grammar, sentence structure and paragraphing. Some students get so tangled up in the jungle of mechanics that they never break through to the creative side. It's not always their fault, either; some teachers are so concerned about mechanical perfection that they brainwash away any creativity which may have been fermenting in those youthful brains.

Some students feel that if they spell correctly and jostle the nouns and verbs into the right neighborhoods, they have done all that can reasonably be expected of them. Other students march to a different drummer; they are sure that teachers with red pencils poised will be so enchanted by gossamer word-webs that spelling and grammar will become irrelevant.

Both groups, I think, are wrong.

Mechanical things matter in the same way that the foundation of a building matters. When you pass a new building, you may be dazzled by its architectural splendor and never give a thought to the foundation, but without the foundation, the building would sink into the swamp.

Creative things matter, too. Oh, my, *how* they matter! A building's foundation may be essential but it is essentially dull. The architect who wants to turn the heads of passersby must give them soaring poetry, too.

Most professional writers don't spend much time thinking about the mechanical foundation of writing. They don't have to; they learned the mechanics early in the game—one might say they made the mechanics "mechanical"—and in their daily work, they are no more likely to think about constructing a proper sentence than a touch typist thinks about striking the letter "e."

How did they achieve this skill? One way, the only way, the hard way, the winner's way—PRACTICE.

HORRIBLE HISTORY

There is a widespread feeling that creativity is something needed mostly by poets and fuzzy people like that. Well, it's true that some kinds of writing do require more creativity than others. More creative juice is needed to write a poem about the onset of spring than to scribble a few cliches on a picture postcard.

In the first case, the poet is trying to stir emotions and establish a mood. In the second case, the writer wants only to gloat to the stay-at-homes or simply announce that he has not been kidnapped.

Does this mean that creativity is required only in poetry or far-out fiction? By no means!

Too many non-fiction writers are crippled by the cozy notion that their only responsibility is to present hard, cold facts, even if that means leaving them there to rot unread on the unturned page. Take history textbooks, for instance . . .

Terrible, aren't they? Dead, dessicated words, trailing off in paragraph after endless paragraph, with no more zip and dash than a telephone directory—statistics, names, dates and places marching along like expired soldiers in a dismal dream. No place for creativity here; it would only slow the muddy flow of facts, right?

Wrong again. There really isn't a lot of dull history; there are only dull historians. History, after all, is no more or less than the record of man's adventures on earth. This is dull? The blood and thunder, upheaval, cruelty, chicanery, suspense, surprises, disasters, suffering, silliness and soaring triumph of man's adventures on earth—this is *dull?*

Well, in most of our history textbooks, it is downright soporific. Small wonder that adults and children alike choose history as their most disliked subject.

What's missing from those books? Creativity, of course. It may be enough merely to set down facts when writing a postcard; it is not nearly enough when writing a history book.

FUN WITH FRENZY

Mechanical, bloodless writing has its place. When you are reading the manual that came with your dune buggy kit, you don't want poetry; you want precision, clarity, conciseness, especially clarity. You want to know how to put the crazy thing together with a minimum of screaming and sweating.

When you are writing a composition for a grade, or a short story for a few quick bucks, or a history textbook, then you also want precision, clarity, conciseness. Which makes manual writing and composition writing pretty much the same . . .

Not on your life!

One very important element is lacking in most manuals that is absolutely essential in a successful composition or short story or history textbook: *emotional impact.*

If you want your reader to turn Nut "A" onto Bolt "B," you have one problem; if you want your reader to laugh or cry or snort or scream, you have quite another problem. If you, as a student, want a teacher to scribble an "A" on a composition in a moment of frenzy, there is only one route to take: emotional impact.

There are a fair number of writers around who can turn out a decent dune buggy manual and I'm afraid there may be some teachers around who like this chilly sort of writing. But why not try for frenzy? It's a lot more fun.

The major defect of much work by inexperienced writers is stiffness. After all, the primary purpose of much writing is self-expression. What do *you* think? How do *you* feel? What do *you* know about a topic that a reader may not? Stiffness is a bad thing because it gets in the way of self-expression.

Envision a speaker addressing a large group. If he or she is frozen with fear of making a mistake or breaking a rule, the speech probably is not going to be effective. It may well be terrible. Until that speaker learns to loosen up and think about the message instead of impending disaster, the message is likely to be lost in a fog of fear.

It is the same with a writer. Until a writer is confident enough to relax, not much exciting writing is likely to flow. But the only way to develop confidence in writing is to write, then write some more. If we wrote as much as we talked, would writing come to feel as natural as talking? Seems possible . . .

It is downright amazing how spoken speech takes on fat when it is written. A student meets another in the hall and says, "Hey, Janey, set committee is meeting at 3 tomorrow in 207. Gotta talk about those lamps. Pass the word, huh?"

Janey decided to turn in a notice for the bulletin and labors to produce this: "The senior stage set committee has scheduled a meeting for Room 207 at 3 o'clock today for discussion about the lighting fixtures. Members of the committee should make sure that everyone on the committee knows about this meeting."

The person in the office who produces the bulletin isn't too excited about that way of putting it, so she rewrites and here's how it comes out next morning: "The chairman of the stage set committee for the senior class play wishes to announce that a meeting will be held at 3 o'clock this afternoon. Lighting fixtures and other matters will be discussed. The meeting will be held in Room 207. The chairman urges all seniors who are members of the committee to take the responsibility of informing all members of the committee about the meeting."

A message that started out with 20 words has been bloated to 67 words and needs to pass through only one more writer's brain before it explodes and sprays fat all over the campus. Is it any wonder that most persons would rather talk than write? And would rather listen than read?

GRAMMAR AND OTHER ANNOYANCES

I promised that this wouldn't turn into a grammar textbook, but I didn't promise that I would ignore the grisly subject.

When you walk into a beautiful building, you usually don't see the steel girders which form its basic structure but you're glad they're there, aren't you? Buildings tend to be heavy and humans aren't squash-proof.

Grammar is simply the basic structure of language.

But it is *only* that, nothing more. Many students, force-fed a heavy diet of grammar rules, lose sight of the fact that grammar is merely a means to an end and the end is communication.

Which comes first, formal grammar or language?

Language, by a long shot. Study of formal grammar is relatively recent; Shakespeare wrote some pretty fair stuff before the study of grammar became popular. Those American founding fathers, whose potent prose is quoted here and there in this book, had little or no formal training in grammar and probably couldn't tell an adjective clause from an anteater.

The development of formal grammar in this country seems to have coincided with the growth of formal education. This makes one suspicious that grammar was primarily important for teaching, rather than for writing. Formal education always seems to work best in subject areas where there is a body of hard fact to pass along. If one is going to teach writing that way, most of one's "hard facts" will have to come from grammar books and then, unfortunately, study of grammar tends to become an end in itself. In fact, our elementary schools once were called "grammar" schools and for all I know, might still be called that in some parts of the country.

Lael Wertenbaker, professional writer, advises students of writing to learn grammar, then forget it. What she means, of course, is that it should be learned well enough and practiced long enough that it becomes second nature, or at least that it can be pushed to the back of the mind. The professional writer may have forgotten the precise rule of grammar which applies in a given situation; all he knows is that what he has just written doesn't sound right. He does not say: "This is obviously because I have violated Rule 47C, Section 2." He says: "Something is wrong. I feel it in my bones. I'll try it this other way and see if it doesn't sound better."

Then he keeps on trying until he finds that better way.

Remember those pick-up games with which we whiled away thousands of golden hours as children? You had an hour before your next meal so you rounded up four or five passersby and began to play. There were no referees or other father figures, but there were rules, generally understood and accepted . . . at first.

In my town, we played by the rules for about 20 minutes, on the average. Then somebody in a fit of pique broke a rule into little bits and from that moment on, law and order slipped out of our grip.

Twenty minutes later, the game had crumbled into chaos. In fact, it had ceased to be a game.

Grammar is like that; without some form of it underlying the whole structure of language, there is no language. A student doesn't diagram sentences to learn how to diagram sentences; he diagrams to become familiar with the structure of language so that when he builds a tower of sentences and steps inside, it won't collapse and flatten him like a bug.

GOOD GRIEF, MORE GRAMMAR

Let us now face up bravely, nose-to-nose, to active and passive verbs.

You learned back about the sixth grade that the active voice of a verb (No, I am not going to explain what a verb is.) occurs when the subject of the verb acts; the passive voice occurs when the subject of the verb is acted upon. Even I can understand that.

Example of active: The boy hit the girl.

Example of passive: The girl was hit by the boy.

That was merely to show you that it is almost always better to use a verb in its active voice than in its passive voice. It's more direct and just plain stronger. (Besides, it saved two words.)

So do it, okay?

CONCRETE AND CANNON BALLS

If there is a single hard-and-fast rule about writing that works (and I'm not sure there is), it is this one:

ALWAYS USE SIMPLE, SPECIFIC, CONCRETE WORDS.

"Ah!" you bleat from the back row, "but suppose I want to write some heady stuff about metaphysics, the kind of prose that touches solid ground only once or twice per page?"

Then by all means use simple, specific, concrete words. The more abstract your idea, the more important it is that you express it simply. Albert Einstein used to write about brain-boggling concepts of physics in clear, simple language. If one couldn't understand his concepts, it was not the fault of his language.

No one can write concisely using woolly, fuzzy words.

Ralph Waldo Emerson said that we should speak what we think in words as hard as cannon balls. Another believer in cannon balls was Benjamin Franklin. In one of those fine writing books published by the federal government, *Gobbledygook Has Gotta Go,* John O'Hayre tells of the battle which raged in Franklin's day over voting rights. Federalists believed that a man ought to own property in order to vote. Franklinites disagreed, to wit:

> "It cannot be adhered to with any reasonable degree of intellectual or moral certainty that the inalienable right man possesses to exercise his political preferences by employing his vote in referendums is rooted in anything other than man's own nature, and is, therefore, properly called a natural right. To hold, for instance, that this natural right can be limited externally by making its exercise dependent on a prior condition of property, is to wrongly suppose that man's natural right to vote is somehow more inherent in and more dependent on the property of man than it is on the nature of man. It is obvious that such belief is unreasonable, for it reverses the order of rights intended by nature."

Now that is a very learned piece of writing but who needs it? Ben Franklin knew that such an argument would convince practically no one and the reason is obvious: far too many abstract words, not nearly enough concrete ones. So he rewrote as follows:

> "To require property of voters leads us to this dilemma: I own a jackass; I can vote. The jackass dies; I cannot vote. Therefore, the vote represents not me but the jackass."

Isn't that beautiful? Words like *cannon balls . . .*

Back in those musty days when queens were really queens, Queen Elizabeth I of England had a problem. A friend of the queen wanted to buy a garden owned by a bishop. The bishop refused to sell, so the queen scribbled a few cannon balls, to wit:

> "Proud Prelate, You know what you were before I made

you what you are now. If you do not immediately comply with my request, I will unfrock you. By God. ELIZABETH."

Pow!

O'Hayre put the principle very well:

> **"If everyone who wrote would put himself in his reader's shoes, at least for a time, then we'd all write a little better and walk a little easier. *Becoming the reader is the essence of becoming a writer."***

DANGER: PUNCTUATION AHEAD

Early writing had no punctuation. (Doesn't that revelation make you tingle?) Then it was discovered that separating sentences with a mark of some sort made reading easier. The next step, as language became more sophisticated, was to insert punctuation within sentences. In modern times, newspaper writers and editors made a strong move back toward simplification of punctuation in order to speed their work. Now modern newspaper style in punctuation is beginning to appear in books and in other "formal" publishing.

Language is changing constantly but if it changes too rapidly, it becomes babble. If it doesn't change at all, it becomes useless. If you don't believe me, pick up a telephone and try to order 100 gallons of fuel oil in Shakespearean English.

Punctuation is not a nuisance; it is a necessity. There have to be fairly rigid rules of punctuation because punctuation works only if it means the same thing all the time. If you make a punctuation mistake, eventually your reader may be able to figure out what you mean if you make the same mistake, in the same way, throughout your piece of writing. But do you really want to be consistent in your *mistakes?*

In the long run, it's easier to try to avoid the mistake in the first place.

FUN AND GAMES WITH COMMAS

I like to use commas to avoid mistaken impressions. Take the sentence: "Inside Dorothy was baking a cake."

Sooner or later a reader would figure out that Dorothy wasn't built like an oven but why make a reader wait when a simple little comma will clear it up?

Sometimes a comma can keep you from making a fool of yourself, too. In *Effective Revenue Writing,* Dr. Calvin D. Linton tells of the radio announcer who read on the air:

"When you are entertaining a full pot of coffee . . ."

He stopped, then considered leaving town by the first plane. The script writer, a former friend, had omitted a comma after "entertaining."

Don't go away; there's more.

"When he swallows his eyes close."

A comma after "swallows" would keep the reader's imagination from running wild.

And consider these intriguing lines of dialogue:

"Come and watch the elephant eat Debbie."

"Come and watch the elephant eat, Debbie."

The first example may be more exciting but if the second meaning was intended, the writer may have a little trouble explaining to the gathering crowd. And he can hardly expect Debbie to help him out.

Every book about writing sooner or later gets around to saying: "Use strong verbs of action whenever possible."

Consider it said in this book. Examples:

"The boy *sat* down on the bench with more than ordinary impact."

"The boy *thumped* down onto the bench."

The second is much stronger than the first and interestingly, it is also shorter. Brevity often leads to strength;

strength often leads to brevity. Why not try to keep that in mind?

MODIFIERS AND OTHER SNEAKS

Rules of language boil down to: "A place for everything and everything in its place." When things get out of place, hilarity, embarassment and even physical damage can result. Let us now consider a tricky devil known as the misplaced modifier.

You know, of course, what a modifier is—a lazy word or phrase which can't stand on its own but must lean on another element in the sentence. Used well, they do for language what salad and dessert do for dinner. Used carelessly, they cause heartburn.

In *Effective Revenue Writing,* Dr. Linton came up with the following burps:

> **"Credit cards shall not be given to customers unless the manager has punched them first."**
>
> **"He will discuss trees, and take the ladies on a tour through the park, identifying them by their shapes and characteristics."**

More, you cry?

A sergeant is showing a not-too-bright recruit how to throw a hand grenade. Says the sergeant: "Now pull the pin and throw it!" The obedient recruit pulls the pin and throws it . . . the pin, that is, while keeping a firm grip on the grenade. *Missing in action . . .*

Care for one more? A man is repairing a tire. He picks up a tire iron, hands a hammer to his friend and says: "I'm going to hold the tire iron against the rim. When I nod my head, hit it."

Such a headache . . .

Phrases used as modifiers can be dangerous; if you give them nothing to modify, they may turn and bite you on the funny bone. The most dangerous place for a modifying phrase is the end of a sentence. To a careless writer, though, the end seems like the logical place to put it. Either he jams it in there ahead of that onrushing period or he must go back and find a better place. Or even, in desperate cases, he must rewrite the sentence.

A careless writer seldom goes back and *never* rewrites, so he comes up with bloopers like these, again quoted from Linton:

> **"There was a discussion held yesterday on the worrying of sheep by dogs in the minister's room."**

(One wishes that weren't a mistake; sounds exciting, if a bit noisy.)

All one has to do to fix that sentence is cut "in the minister's room" off the end of the sentence and squeeze it in after "yesterday."

Here's another, this time from a radio announcer:

> **"Stay tuned in and I'll be back and tell you how to spend six weeks in Hawaii in a minute."**

What a great vacation for a busy executive!

Another dangerous spot for a modifier is the beginning of a sentence, where you can get into this kind of trouble:

> **"Moving high in the sky and emitting a loud whooshing sound, my husband and I saw a silver, cigar-shaped object in the sky."**

That sounds like a lot of fun but some sober citizen is certain to point out that introductory phrase is obviously in the wrong place and would we please come down to earth and stop whooshing?

This notice was posted on the bulletin board of an Irish golf club:

> **"Trousers are now allowed to be worn by ladies on the**

course. But they must be removed before entering the clubhouse."

That's the way it is with words—take your eye off them for a second and they get out of hand. Moral: Read what you have written before you post it on the bulletin board . . . or anywhere else.

And here's an intriguing sentence:

> **"Having devoured our dinner, the train pulled out of the station."**

Now everybody knows what was meant by that sentence. After all, trains don't steal food. But with no personal pronoun for "Having devoured our dinner" to modify, the sentence accuses this particular train of the crime. Readers shouldn't have to dig out meaning from a sentence; a sentence should come right out and say what it means.

Be kind to railroads; take a locomotive to lunch today.

My alltime favorite misplaced modifier, the world's champion, is this one:

> **"In accordance with your instructions, I have given birth to twins in the enclosed envelope."**

SOMETHING TO THINK ABOUT

A very common grammar mistake is made by millions of persons every day while they are straining to be correct. They use the phrase "between you and I." Sounds very prim and proper, doesn't it?

It's dead wrong. "I" can't be used as the object of the preposition "between." The correct phrase is "between you and me." Sometimes a mistake is repeated so often that it becomes part of the language. My guess is that not one person in 10 would pick the correct form in this case.

Another example, is "I couldn't care less." Through

some mysterious process, this became "I *could* care less," even though it has precisely the opposite meaning of the first phrase! "I could care less" even pops out of the mouths of television announcers who are being paid to know better. "I could care less" is a perfectly correct sentence, of course, but isn't it pretty silly to use it when what you mean is that you couldn't care less? Let very much of this kind of thing creep into a language and it becomes worthless babble.

WORD PLAY

Watch out for ambiguity. What's that, you ask? Unclear meanings or meanings you don't intend. Lyle M. Crist, author of *Man Expressed: The Realm of Writing,* came up with this rummage sale notice from a newspaper:

> **"The ladies of the Maple Street Church have discarded clothing of all kinds. They invite everyone to come in and inspect them."**

And another, from a newspaper advertisement: "All skirts will be half off tomorrow . . ."

See? Words can be tricky. Amusing, but tricky.

SOMETHING TO WRITE

Write a paragraph of about 100 words concerning the last thing that made you very angry. Make sure that you have punctuated it properly. Then rewrite it without any punctuation at all. That's right; none at all. Read it carefully to yourself, then aloud.

Sort of a mess, isn't it?

"A mass of Latin words falls upon the facts like soft snow blurring the outlines and covering up all the details. The great enemy of clear language is insincerity. When there is a gap between one's real and one's declared aims, one turns instinctively to long words, and exhausted idioms, like a cuttlefish squirting out ink."

—George Orwell

5. Come Right Out and Say It

When you talk to another person, you get an immediate reaction to your message—a frown, a smile, a snort, a punch in the mouth.

When you communicate by writing, reaction is usually delayed. Right there, I think, is the most important difference between writing and talking.

If you don't make yourself clear when you speak, your listener has several ways of letting you know right now. He might even snap: "Say that again in plain English, knot-head."

Writers must never forget this striking difference between the written message and the spoken message. When writing, they must be especially careful to say exactly what they mean in terms readers can understand readily, because there will be no instant feedback. In fact, it is entirely possible for a writer to lose an audience with the first paragraph and not become aware of it until he discovers three days later that the dam actually did burst and those unfortunate souls he tried to warn with his wordy telegram were washed to a watery death.

Better to make your written messages simple and clear than to be responsible for the untimely exit of persons who may owe you money.

THE CUTTLEFISH SQUIRTS

It's amazing how many simple, unpretentious, straightforward persons turn into pompous asses when they sit down to write. In *Gobbledygook Has Gotta Go,* John O'Hayre offers good examples of the sickness, the first one in a report from a state fire warden:

> **"FIRE REPORT: Heavy rains throughout most of the state have given an optimistic outlook for lessened fire danger for the rest of the season. However, an abundance of lightning maintains a certain amount of hazard in isolated areas that have not received an excessive amount of rain. We were pleased to have been able to help Nevada with the suppression of their conflagration."**

According to O'Hayre, the man who wrote that gummy paragraph is an educated, plain-talking fellow. But look at how he writes! The paragraph was rewritten by someone good at filtering out fog, with the following result:

> **"Fire readings are down throughout most of the state.**

But a few rain-skipped areas are dry, and lightning is a hazard there. We are glad we could send some of our people to help Nevada put out their recent range fire."

Sixty stuffy words shrunk to 42 plain ones and think how much more comfortable you'd feel if you were one of those Nevada citizens, knowing that somebody could help put out your fires, even if they couldn't suppress your conflagrations.

President Franklin D. Roosevelt was a very effective writer and speaker. During World War II, an important man in government sent the President the following memo concerning the actions of federal workers in case of an air raid:

"Such preparations shall be made as will completely obscure all Federal buildings and non-Federal buildings occupied by the Federal Government during an air raid for any period of time from visibility by reason of internal or external illumination. Such obscuration may be obtained either by blackout construction or by termination of illumination."

Roosevelt knew that by the time government workers deciphered that glob of goop, the air raid would be over, so he rewrote it: "Tell them that in buildings where they have to keep the work going to put something over the windows; and, in buildings where they can let the work stop for awhile, turn out the lights."

A pompous writer is almost always a bad writer who is trying to conceal his fault. He usually fools only one person: himself.

Clarity equals communication. If there is a formula for good writing, there it is. One of the major obstacles to clarity is a little word called "pronoun." Here is an example of some roadblocks in a question to a newspaper advice column:

> **"When a married couple has a will, and the husband dies, in which he left some to his mother, is it paid or must it be left until the wife dies.**
>
> **—Name Withheld."**

The answer: "There is no way to answer this without knowing the exact wording of the will. A competent lawyer should be consulted."

Humbug! There is no way to answer this without knowing the exact wording of the *question.* Even a "competent lawyer" would have trouble figuring out what that puzzled person wanted to know. There are at least three serious problems of communication presented by this dazzling question.

One—it should be at least three sentences, not one. Two—the syntax is terrible. That is to say, one thought does not lead logically into another. Three—the *pronouns* protrude; a pair of two-letter words dealt that question a death blow: "he" and "it." Pronouns, both of them.

The grammar books say that a pronoun is supposed to refer to a noun which precedes it and the pronoun must agree with the noun in gender and number. Long sentences often demand many pronouns; often pronouns can be eliminated by shortening sentences. Let's rewrite that question:

> **"A married couple has a will and the husband dies. The will left a legacy to the husband's mother. Should the legacy be paid immediately or can the legacy wait until the wife dies?"**

Three sentences instead of one. No pronouns. The question is now clear, right?

It isn't?

Perhaps you should consult a competent lawyer.

ZSA ZSA AND THE JEWEL THIEF

Communication is affected not only by the amount of material one tries to stuff into a sentence but also by *where* one tries to stuff it. Consider this intriguing example from a newspaper:

> **"NEW YORK—Zsa Zsa Gabor was held up at gunpoint early Wednesday in an elevator of the Waldorf-Towers where she lives and robbed of more than $600,000 worth of jewels, the hotel said."**

Now let's consider that little masterpiece. I can read that paragraph three times and have it come out twice that Zsa Zsa lives in an elevator. I doubt that very much. Let's do a rewrite:

> **"NEW YORK—Zsa Zsa Gabor was held up at gunpoint early Wednesday in the Waldorf-Towers and robbed of more than $600,000 worth of jewels.**
>
> **"The actress lives in the hotel. The robbery took place in an elevator."**

That's clear, isn't it? What may have confused me is the last three words of the original quote: ". . . the hotel said." When hotels speak, they often garble the message.

Speaking of garbled messages, here's one which also appeared in a newspaper; the author is professor of business administration at a prestigious university:

> **"Neither the poet nor the ad man celebrates the literal functionality of what he produces. Instead, each celebrates a deep and complex emotion which he symbolizes by creative embellishment—a content which cannot be captured by literal description alone. Communication, through advertising or through poetry or any other medium, is a creative conceptualization that implies a vicarious experience through a language of symbolic substitutes. Communication can never be the real thing it talks about. Therefore,**

all communications are in some inevitable fashion a departure from reality."

The headline over that lump of wordage was "Quote Worth Repeating." Go ahead; repeat it; I dare you. What the man was talking about, incidentally, was "communication." I know because I wrote and asked him.

While it's open season on newspapers, try this lead paragraph from one:

> **"A slim 52 per cent victory in 94 per cent of the statewide vote on the cigarette tax referendum was indicated by the time the last polling place in Metzer County completed the negative vote count cast by all 25 polling units."**

Now there is a paragraph that is packed with information to the slop-over point. No wasted words, right? Or were they all wasted? One wonders if a single mind can absorb it all. Probably not without reading the sentence three times, then swinging toward Mecca and praying for guidance.

Never waste words; this is a cardinal rule; use only as many as necessary, then cut a few. But a sentence is not a camel; don't break its back with an overload of information.

What I'm wondering is: Did that cigarette tax referendum pass? Or did that negative vote count do it in? One thing you have to say for bad writing is that it sustains suspense.

There is a widespread belief that the most important requirement for writing is that it be "correct." That does matter, of course, but isn't it more important that writing be *effective?*

That American patriot could have said: "It appears to me at this climactic point in history that I am faced with a choice between my cherished freedoms and my mortal existence; I would prefer to lose the latter rather than the former."

That's correct, isn't it?

But what Patrick Henry actually said was: "Give me liberty or give me death!"

That's correct, too, but it's also effective. This paper-plastered world is choked with "correct" writing that is either putting people to sleep or boggling their minds. It is a good thing to be correct; it is a much better thing to be effective. Why not shoot for both?

Government writing has a way of being correct without being effective. Consider this lead paragraph from a Department of Interior publication:

> "One of the Department of the Interior's largest reclamation projects is the Columbia Basin project in Washington. A multipurpose irrigation, power, and flood control development utilizing a portion of the resources of the Columbia River, it is situated in the central part of the State. Its key feature is massive 350-foot-high Grand Coulee Dam, which is capable of impounding 9.4 million acre-feet of water in Franklin D. Roosevelt Lake, has an installed nameplate capacity of 1,974,000 kilowatts in its powerplant, and is expected to eventually furnish irrigation water for over a million acres of land."

There's as much cement in that paragraph as there is in that dam. Surely, with one of the wonders of the world to write about, the writer could have come up with a zippier opening. Not only is it dull; it assaults the reader with far too many figures. Let's try the same subject, Grand Coulee Dam, but with a different writer:

> "It is just possible that a few persons doing no more than standing and sweating and holding up signs on a dusty road in eastern Washington changed the face of the state forever

and won a world war.

"Before you scoff, consider these facts:

"The year was 1934. The road led to the site of a low dam being built on the Columbia River near the huge, ancient trench known as Grand Coulee. The signs were blunt: 'WE WANT THE HIGH DAM!'"

Isn't that better? *I* think it is because I wrote it for a state of Washington history book. What's your excuse?

The interesting, colorful, lively word is always a better choice than the dull, ordinary, much-used one. For example, it would be easy to write a phrase like "giving an alarm." With a little more effort, you could make it "roaring out an alarm." The single effect of those few words is not great, but multiply that effect by 100 in a 1000-word piece of writing and you might turn a weak story into a strong one.

EDITING THE BIBLE

The 23rd Psalm is often pointed to as one of the most beautiful pieces of writing in the Bible. In case you've forgotten, it runs along like this:

"The Lord is my shepherd; I shall not want.

"He maketh me to lie down in green pastures: he leadeth me beside the still waters.

"He restoreth my soul: he leadeth me in the paths of righteousness for his name's sake.

"Yea, though I walk through the valley of the shadow of death, I will fear no evil: for thou art with me; thy rod and thy staff they comfort me.

"Thou preparest a table before me in the presence of mine enemies: thou anointest my head with oil; my cup runneth over.

"Surely goodness and mercy shall follow me all the days of my life: and I will dwell in the house of the Lord for ever."

Sure, that's great writing. But the language is archaic, for one thing. Would it mean a whole lot to children as it stands? To an Indian child on a reservation in Arizona, let's say?

According to Cook Christian Training School, Tempe, Arizona, this is the Indian version:

> **"The Great father above a shepherd is. I am His and with Him I want not. He throws out to me a rope and the name of the rope is love and He draws me to where the grass is green and the water not dangerous, and I eat and lie down and am satisfied. Sometimes my heart is very weak and falls down, but He lifts me up again and draws me into a good road. His name is Wonderful."**

Now isn't that something special?

Effective writing can occur in strange places. Some of the most effective these days appears on bumper stickers. I am driving up the street minding my own business one day when a bumper sticker on the van in front hits me between the eyes: "HONK—IF YOU LOVE JESUS." Talk about tight, punchy writing!

Come to think of it, though, nobody honked. (As a paid-up member of the counter-culture, I intend to have this sticker printed: "HONK — IF JESUS LOVES NOISE POLLUTION.")

One of my favorite historical characters is Satchel Paige, a great black baseball player, raconteur and free-lance philosopher. Because of his color, Paige came to the major leagues late but hung around for a while until he became the oldest player ever to perform in the majors. (Some doubt may be cast on this, since Paige was always coy about his age.)

Paige became a public figure (and eventually a member of the Baseball Hall of Fame) not only because of his baseball ability but because of his skill at expressing himself simply and effectively. Here are some of Paige's rules for eternal youth:

"If your stomach disputes you, lie down and pacify it with cool thoughts."

"Avoid fried meats, which angry up the blood."

"Keep the juices flowing by jangling gently as you move."

"Avoid running at all times."

"Don't look back. Something may be gaining on you."

I ask you: Could professional psychologists, dieticians and philosophers say it half as well? Simplicity is beautiful.

SOMETHING TO THINK ABOUT

Did it ever occur to you that everyone has three vocabularies? The largest is made up of words we recognize in print. Second, words we use in writing. Third—and by far the smallest—words we use in talking.

But those three vocabularies aren't frozen. Usually we first encounter a new word in print, then later use it in writing and finally, in a very few cases, we fit the word into our talking vocabulary.

SOMETHING TO WRITE

Cliches are words and phrases which are worn out from being overworked. In his book, *Good Writing,* Alan H. Vrooman concocted a paragraph made up entirely of cliches to describe a sudden rain at a picnic:

"Mother Nature was in all her glory, but by the irony of fate we were doomed to disappointment. After all has been said, in the last analysis the raging elements can always nip our hopes in the bud and with one fell swoop wreak havoc upon any festive occasion."

Everyone has favorite cliches. What are yours? Write a paragraph using as many as you can think of.

Then give the tired old things a proper funeral.

SOMETHING MORE TO THINK ABOUT

"Language is primarily the thing we think with; it is more than mere communication."

—Harold E. Palmer

Isn't that interesting? Some time when you feel like beating your head against the wall, try to think about something—anything—without using words.

How did human beings think before the development of formal language? How do animals think? They do, you know.

Do Siamese cats born and raised in France think in French? Do Siamese cats born and raised in England think in English? Or do they both think in Siamese?

Which came first, language or thought?

"I am sorry for the length of my letter, but I had not the time to write a short one."

—Blaise Pascal

6. Rules and Rubbish

Sooner or later (usually sooner), a student of writing picks up a book which tells him that if he will just follow the printed rules, 1 through 17 (or 71), he will be able to write a theme that will blow his teacher's wig right through the ceiling.

One man's rules are another man's rubbish.

You can't write successfully with one eye on a book of

rules any more than you can operate a car safely while holding an open driver's manual in one hand.

And it doesn't help much to memorize the rules, then pick the applicable one from the back of your mind as you need it in your writing. Too bad; that would be so much easier than *thinking*. But writing *is* thinking, and all the rules in the world can't alter that hard fact. Anyone who tries to substitute rules for thought is headed down a blind alley.

You *can* use rules as yardsticks when you revise what you have written. If you have a problem with over-long sentences, for instance, don't count words while writing; save the arithmetic for later. Once started writing, you should let nothing slow you down. Momentum is enormously important; distractions can be deadly. You have been warned.

Picture a student sitting down to write and thinking: "Now I do this, he says, and now I do that, he says, and then I go on to this, and . . ."

I don't think good writing can happen that way. The student who tries to write that way is going to wind up with a head full of rules and precious little on paper that is worth reading. (You may have a teacher who thinks otherwise; there are some of those around. The teacher may be right; I may be wrong; we should all think about it.)

Take similes and metaphors, for instance. Some writing textbooks will tell you in great detail what similes and metaphors are, then will give you examples, then will assign you to sit down and dash off a few. Maybe it can be done that way but most of the professional writers I know, who write similes and metaphors every day, can't tell one from a giraffe. And what's more, they never could. To professionals, similes and metaphors are merely ways of arranging words to suit a certain situation. The professional uses them when they sound right to his trained ear. And how do you train ears? By reading and writing, not by learning rules and trying too diligently to follow them as you write.

And the next rule is . . .

BICYCLES AND NOSEBLEEDS

The trouble with making flat rules about writing is that as soon as you do it, you have to make flat exceptions.

Short sentences are good, excellent, the best. But even with strawberry shortcake, one can get a bellyful. Short sentences combined with a few long ones provide the rhythmic flow which keeps a reader's eyes dancing along the page. Take a paragraph like this:

> "The bicycle was moving slowly on the sidewalk. The boy riding the bicycle had a nosebleed. He was crying, too, and rubbing his nose. A car stopped by the bicycle. A man asked the boy what he was crying about. The boy said he always got nosebleeds on Tuesday. He was crying because he was bleeding all over his new bicycle. The man in the car said, 'But this is Wednesday,' and drove away. The boy rode his bicycle into a brick wall. He stopped crying because he was mad at the wall. He stopped bleeding because it was Wednesday."

(It occurs to me that I may just have written the beginning of a book for six-year-olds. Remember the incredible writing in those books?)

Look at all the short, simple sentences in that paragraph, then consider how choppy and jerky it is. There must be more to good writing than short, simple sentences. Let's rewrite, varying the length and type of sentences:

> "Riding slowly along the sidewalk on his bicycle, the boy cried and rubbed his nose, which was bleeding. A car stopped near the bicycle and a man in the car asked the boy why he was crying. The man also asked him why he was bleeding. He was crying, the boy said, because he was getting blood all over his new bicycle. He was bleeding, he added, because Tuesday was his day for nosebleeds. 'But this is Wednesday,' said the man in the car, just before driving away. Then the boy rode his bicycle into a brick

wall. Angry at the wall, he stopped crying. Now aware that it was Wednesday, he also stopped bleeding."

Now this gripping account of the boy and his bicycle has lost much of the water torture effect of the first paragraph. It *flows* much better, doesn't it? The name of the game is rhythm.

Alas, rewritten, the paragraph is just as silly as ever. All I promised you was rhythm, not a miracle.

Good, graphic writing consists of painting word pictures. A writer shouldn't attempt to tell a reader what he has seen; he should let the reader see for himself and draw his own conclusions. Here's how a writer tells a reader what the reader has seen:

> **"The old man was tired, defeated. He wanted only to be free of his troubles forever; only his concern for the dog beside him kept him alive. Life was ending, but in that moment seemed endless."**

Now let's paint a picture instead:

> **"The wizened man dragged his crippled leg, stirring dust in the evening sunlight spilling across the empty road. With lowered head, he shuffled onward into nowhere. Then, with a strong effort, he straightened and fondly touched the head of the dog beside him. 'Some time left,' he muttered. 'Mebbe too much.' "**

It is always more effective to project a picture onto a screen than to tell someone what the picture would have looked like if it had been projected. True, you can bore your friends by showing home movies but you can lose them forever by *not* showing home movies and merely telling them what they missed.

It is possible to get so badly mired down in a sentence

that there is no escape. In this emergency, don't try to slog across the swamp; return to the near shore and make a fresh beginning. After all, you're not engraving words in stone; it's a lot easier to wipe them out than it was to write them.

PUNCH IN A PARAGRAPH

It is dangerous these days to make rules about paragraphing, or even to define "paragraph." Increasingly, in modern writing, a paragraph is what the writer says it is.

But if I were forced to tiptoe in the direction of making rules about paragraphing, they would be something like this:

Don't waste the beginning and ending of a paragraph, because these are the most emphatic places. If you want to give a particular statement or piece of information special punch, put it at the beginning of a paragraph or at the end.

If you want to be *really* emphatic, use a one-sentence paragraph, like this one.

It's been said before and it's worth saying again: It always adds strength to write in specific terms. Strong writing uses specific words, not general ones. By the same token, concrete words are more powerful than abstract ones.

General: *A woman was talking to her husband.*

Specific: *Angry Alice screamed at cowering George.*

Abstract: *She expressed her anger in a violent way.*

Concrete: *Alice whacked George solidly with a broom.*

The second version is much stronger than the first in each case. Don't take my word for it; ask George.

Textbooks on writing, while varying generally, seem to agree on a few principles; following are three which pop up again and again:

BE CLEAR. Clarity is the first and last goal of good writing. Those who do not write understandably are cheating readers and there is always the suspicion that they write murkily because they really don't know what they are writing about but want to conceal the fact.

USE SHORT SENTENCES AND SHORT WORDS. Now, of course, this doesn't mean that a long sentence is necessarily a bad one nor that a long word is necessarily a bad one. Sentence variety adds rhythm to writing. Some excellent writers are able to write very long sentences which are entirely clear. For most writers, however, it is better to use many more short sentences than long ones. The same principle can be applied to paragraphs. In much newspaper writing, one-sentence paragraphs are common and seldom does a paragraph contain more than three sentences. Use of many short paragraphs give a brightness and lightness to the printed page, enhancing readability.

DON'T WASTE WORDS. Do not repeat yourself, unless you have a very good reason. If one word will get your meaning across, don't use two. It might be a good idea for student writers to devote one complete revision of their work to cutting excess words.

DOT, DOT, DOT

If I am ever asked to judge a beauty contest for punctuation marks, I'll vote early and often for the period. This quiet little dot is a dandy. Take a deep breath and read this sentence:

> "We appear recently to have taken a precious human right, the right to dissent, a right which is, and has been, available to all men and at all times, a right which is both eloquent and powerful in its expression, a right which certain religious and political leaders throughout all ages of man's history have exercised only under the most extreme conditions involving strong personal conviction and then only with full knowledge of its use as an instrument of despair and with full knowledge that its use clearly will quite likely not, or will not immediately, lead to a reversal of the majority, and we have seen this precious right of

dissent exercised so often recently and without acknowledging its true cost that we have almost perverted it into a license for anarchy and treason without labeling it as such (as did, for example, Patrick Henry and Joan of Arc)."

Isn't that incredible? An extreme example, granted, but swamps as deep as that await the unwary writer. Reading that particular marathon effort makes me want to take a pailful of periods and just slosh them over the whole gooey mess.

Judges and lawyers have their own verbal smog. If they wrote clearly most of the time, we wouldn't need so many judges and lawyers, which may have something to do with it. Consider this paragraph from a legal opinion:

> **"The trial court canceled the deeds from Webb to Stewart and Cascadia on the ground the deed from Webb to Stewart had been fraudulently induced, but held that Wilson acted in good faith and without notice of the fraud when she accepted the trust deed as security for her loan and therefore held her deed to be a prior and valid lien on plaintiff's property."**

Whew! Are you still with me? Then please tell me where we are. There's nothing too difficult about the legal jargon in that paragraph and it would be hard to find a single excess word. So why is it so difficult to understand? Simply because it's all one sentence. Let's break it up:

> **"The trial court cancelled the deeds from Webb to Stewart and Cascadia on the ground the deed from Webb to Stewart had been fraudulently induced. But the court also held that Wilson acted in good faith and without notice of the fraud when she accepted the trust deed as security for her loan. Therefore the court held her deed to be a prior and valid lien on plaintiff's property."**

I told you periods are wonderful, probably the greatest

invention since peanut butter.

Since we started out in this chapter talking about rules, let me throw in one last rule: *Let rules be your yardstick, but not your crutch.*

WORD PLAY

The problem is to write an eleven-word sentence using "that" five times, all in a row. Not easy, but here it is:

"I said that that 'that' that that man used was incorrect."

You may want to repeat that a few times.

MORE WORD PLAY

An old story:

Two priests argued whether it was proper to smoke and pray at the same time. One said yes, the other no. They decided to write to the Pope for his opinion.

Eventually each received a reply; each insisted that the Pope had supported his view. One asked: "How did you phrase your question?"

Replied the other: "I asked whether it was proper to smoke while one is praying, and the Pope answered, 'Certainly not, praying is serious business and permits of no distractions.' And how did you phrase your question?"

Said the other: "I asked if it were proper to pray while smoking, and the Pope said, 'Certainly, prayer is always in order.' "

How you say it makes all the difference.

SOMETHING TO REMEMBER

Bedfellows: SHORTNESS—SIMPLICITY—STRENGTH.

"When I say writing, O, believe me, it is rewriting that I have chiefly in mind."

—Robert Louis Stevenson

7. Fishing Season Never Closes

"I was born while my mother was tied to the railroad tracks two miles out of Perth Amboy, N.J., with a milk train only half a mile away and my father doing a lot of screaming and yelling."

Intrigued you, didn't I? I also faked you right out of your socks because the first paragraph is a phony. Yes, Virginia, there is a Perth Amboy, N.J., but the truth is, I was born in a highly conventional manner in Montevideo, Minnesota.

All of which is meant to illustrate a simple point: The first paragraph is the most important in anything you write; it is the hook on your fishing line, small but potent. The rest of your fishing gear might have cost $400 but if that two-bit hook fails you, forget the fish.

It should come as no surprise, then, that the term usually used by professional writers in referring to that catchy beginning is "hook."

Since time began, English teachers have faced a new class and bravely uttered: "Your first assignment will be an autobiography." (I did that when I was teaching English and I'll tell you why. Students usually find it easy to write about themselves because no other subject is so fascinating; and besides, no research is needed. Also, autobiographies give a teacher a quick line on a new bunch of faces which can be acquired no other way. If I have given away a trade secret, it's no big deal; this book is full of them.)

Since time began, students have plunged into the first paragraph of that first theme and inevitably have come up with a variation of this opening sentence: "I was born in Cedar Falls, Iowa, on September 21, 1959, in a brick hospital but I don't really remember much about it because I was so young." (The last clause of that sentence is always included by the class clown.)

Since time began, teachers have attacked a pile of those predictable papers with unmuffled groans. If I accomplish nothing else with this book, I hope that I slice off a few from the vast mass of students who start an autobiographical theme in that way. If I manage that, English teachers will write me in for President.

Do I have to explain what's wrong with that first paragraph? No hook—it's DULL, DULL, DULL. A bored teacher is not a happy teacher; only a happy teacher is going to give you the grade you want on an autobiography or any other writing assignment.

Let's throw out that beginning forever unless you can

honestly write something like the first paragraph of this chapter or:

> **"I was born in a basket under a gas bag floating at 2000 feet over Anchorage, Alaska, and the bag was leaking."**

Moses in the bullrushes isn't bad, either, but it's been used.

I have a friend who writes and sells short fiction. One story was entitled "My Baby Was Born on a Roller Coaster." Honest! Wouldn't that make a great beginning for an autobiographical theme? You just know the teacher would read on. Don't guffaw too hard at that title, incidentally; it was worth several hundred dollars to my friend.

No matter what you write, begin it well and you're halfway home. I believe this and practice it when I write history textbooks. I try hard to put a hook in every opening paragraph of every chapter. I was delighted to be able to open a chapter of a book called *Washington Times and Trails* in this fashion:

> **"On the evening of December 30, 1905, a man named Frank Steunenberg opened his garden gate in Caldwell, Idaho, and in the next instant was blown to kingdom come."**

Of course, you can't always expect to come up with material as graphic as that; not that many people get blown up. But if you work at it, you can always find something that will spark up that first paragraph. You will be glad you did, and so will your glassy-eyed teacher facing yet another hilarious weekend of theme reading.

HOW TO STROKE A CAT

Now that you'll never again write a dull opening paragraph, you might inscribe another little tip on the soft part of your brain: *Don't load more information into the first paragraph than it can carry comfortably on a weak back.*

Remembering this can help a great deal in making your opening lively. Once a writer friend sent me an article he had written (and published) and asked for criticism. Here is the first paragraph:

> **"Along a five mile avenue of sorrow stretching from the Moore Memorial Church in Shanghai to Jungjoa Airdrome, a funeral procession moved bearing the body of Colonel Robert Short, American. The date was April 25, 1932. Two months previously, on Washington's birthday, the 27-year-old pilot had heroically given his life to China in a one-sided air battle against the Japanese. As the cortege made its way slowly down the old Tibet Road, tens of thousands of Chinese stood in silent tribute. Following the hearse were forty-five cars laden with floral pieces, and some three hundred cars carrying the greats of China, including T.V. Soong, Minister. At graveside four thousand Chinese, in mixtures of Oriental and Occidental dress paid final respects. It was the largest and most impressive funeral ever accorded a foreigner in China."**

Names, places, dates . . . an enormous load of information, nearly all of it interesting. I rewrote that paragraph, then said to my friend: "As you will see, I used much the same material you did, just rearranged it a little. I feel that you try to include too much information in the first few paragraphs and it gets a little too heavy for the reader. One shouldn't give him too much to absorb immediately; load him up slowly. I believe in short paragraphs and not only in the lead. Newspaper writing develops this habit; notice that many paragraphs in a news story are only one sentence long. This gives the type a light, easily-read look."

Here is the rewritten paragraph:

> **"Tens of thousands of Chinese lined the avenue of sorrow as the cortege passed on a spring day in 1932; four thousand more appeared at Jungjoa Airdrome to offer tribute at graveside.**

"The cortege which had rolled slowly from Moore Memorial Church in Shanghai was composed of the hearse, 45 flower-laden cars and 300 more vehicles carrying the leaders of China, including T.V. Soong, Minister.

"The state funeral honored a national hero of China . . . but a man who was not Chinese.

"He was Robert McCawley Short, American.

"More exactly, Colonel Robert Short, American pilot who had died in air battle defending China against the Japanese."

Now I think that's better, but I'm prejudiced. In my version, the information is spoon-fed to the reader. The objective at this early point is to inform him just a little, intrigue him a lot. Once hooked, a reader can be loaded up with information; he may even like it then. It's much like letting a strange cat smell your fingers before you try to stroke its fur.

A reader will put up with a lot and still fight on, but he won't put up with *dullness* for very long. A writer must intrigue a reader, bait him, anger him, amuse him, titillate him, inform him, educate him, startle him . . . but never *bore* him. A writer who bores a reader soon loses a reader in this world full of fascinating distractions. You might remember that. Professional writers remember that or, to keep from starving, they go to work in the postoffice.

GOING THROUGH THE GEARS

Professional writers, as a group, tend to look down on teachers of writing, as a group; they also sneer softly at writers employed by government. They shouldn't look down for a moment on a particular teacher of writing who is also a government writing consultant. I refer again to Dr. Calvin D. Linton, who wrote this pithy paragraph in *Effective Revenue Writing:*

"Every reader who picks up a piece of writing is starting

out on a journey. Unlike most travelers, however, he is entirely dependent on someone else to tell him why he is going, where he is going, and how he is going to get there. These things only the writer knows, and as likely as not he's not talking. If he is an average, nonprofessional writer, that is. But if he has ever had to make his living by putting one word after another on a piece of paper, he knows that it is helpful to make his writing correct, gratifying to make it stylistically pleasing, profitable to make it interesting, but absolutely mandatory to make it clear and sequential. He knows that of all the timid creatures of the deep forest, the reader is the timidest, the most likely to sniff the bait from about a hundred yards away and then disappear. If the bait (the first sentence) is not outstandingly toothsome, if the next little bite is not hooked to it, and the next to that, and so on until the doors of the trap (the conclusion) snap shut on the furry little creature (the . . . reader, of course), the hunter may as well give up hunting and become a supervisor or a top administrator. Best of all, he can become a teacher of writing."

There, in a single paragraph, is the key to effective writing.

In Linton's book, the writer-reader relationship is presented graphically in a tantalizing diagram:

Meshing gears often squawk, squeal and whine. The more flaws they have, the more noise they make. If the gear at the left—the mind of the writer—has flaws, the abrasion will grind some flaws into the middle gear—the writing itself. Since the two gears at the left are always flawed, there is certain to be some squawking from the gear at the right—the reader. And, of course, the gear at the right always has a few flaws of its own, thus adding to the uproar when the machine is running.

The writer who is aware of his reader's problems can squirt a little oil on certain cogs of that gear to the right to reduce the noise pollution.

When the left gear revolves, the others must revolve with it. (This is known in physics as "Revolver's Law.") But what is to prevent the right gear from simply stopping and thereby dragging the others to a grinding halt?

Nothing. It happens all the time. A writer must never forget that a reader has this power. When a reader's cogs get out of joint, the whole process stops. Then those two gears at the left can be sold for rusty junk.

Moral: Writers shouldn't spare the oil.

SOMETHING TO WRITE

Look at the opening paragraphs of your last three themes. Is there a hook in any of them? Are they too long? Do they present too much information too fast?

Shame on you. Rewrite them, adding all the zing at your command. If you are temporarily short on zing, borrow some or fake it. Writers are often driven to desperate measures.

"Alice had not the slightest idea what Latitude was, or Longitude either, but she thought they were nice grand words to say."

—Lewis Carroll

8. The Sound of Smog

A child will say: "Do it again."

An adult will say: "Repeat the experiment, please."

The gobbledygook expert will write: "It was determined to replicate the experiment."

The kid was the one who really communicated.

You can write: "Simians indigenous to Zamboanga are destitute of caudal appendages."

Or you can transmit the same message by writing: "Monkeys have no tails in Zamboanga."

I don't suppose monkeys care which you write . . . but readers do. Why make monkeys of your readers?

Students rarely write gobbledygook. The disease usually strikes at the beginning of middle age, when the patient's waist begins to thicken and the brain begins to ossify and the self-image shows signs of terminal bloat. But it is worthwhile for students to become aware of the disease and its symptoms, because only early awareness can prevent it. To date, no vaccine has been developed; only careful nurture of the developing brain can stave off the dread malady.

Gobbledygook is definitely contagious. In fact, in some areas of government, it is a raging epidemic. What do you suppose the Bureau of Public Roads calls those oil drums placed around highway obstacles? "Impact attenuation devices," that's what. When is a parachute not a a parachute? When it's an "aerodynamic personnel decelerator," that's when, and the army so labels it.

Infected by examples like those, Eric Allen, editor of the *Medford Mail Tribune* (Oregon) suggested that we call stop lights "electronically actuated color-coded vehicular flow control mechanisms."

Now let's hear it for the U.S. Navy, which has been known to report that a ship loaded with "fossil fuels" was being bothered because of "motion caused by a climatic disturbance at the sea-air interface."

Translation: "An oil tanker is in trouble because of high waves." So why not come right out and say so?

A person who calls a spade a spade has always been known as a plain-talker, right? Sort of a John Wayne type. Then the plain-talker ran afoul of Selective Service and was handed a "combat emplacement evacuator." This is army talk for "shovel." Honest. John Wayne would never say a thing like that.

ALWAYS A TROUBLEMAKER

Once upon a time there strode in the marble halls of

government an official who decided that efficiency would be improved if his staff wrote shorter memos. He asked his assistant to write and circulate a memo to that effect; it was done.

The assistant's memo was received and read by an anonymous troublemaker in the government service, who decided that the word count of the memo asking for shorter memos was about three times as high as it needed to be. So the troublemaker rewrote the memo, and circulated his effort.

The original memo began like this: "As a general rule, and certainly not applicable to all situations, the briefing memoranda forwarded to the Secretary have been loaded with an excess amount of verbiage."

The troublemaker's translation: "Most of the briefing memoranda forwarded to the Secretary have been too wordy."

Next paragraph of the original memo: "In the future the briefing memoranda should highlight the issue, set forth alternative courses of action or approaches to resolve the issue, and finally, a recommendation regarding the action to be taken by the Secretary should be made with reasons therefor."

Translation from troublemaker: "Briefing memoranda should highlight the issue, state alternatives to resolve the issue, and the action to be taken by the Secretary."

The original memo's next paragraph: "It is envisioned that this sort of writing will not require more than a page and a half to two pages at the most."

Troublemaker: "No more than two pages should be required."

There was more in a similar vein, but in the interest of "shorter briefing memoranda," I won't go on.

Moral No. 1: If you have something to say, say it, and quit messing around. If you have nothing to say, say it in fewer words.

Moral No. 2: You, too, can be a troublemaker.

Many specialized areas of government have communications problems. They need to get through to the taxpaying public but apparently nobody on their payrolls speaks English. Take aviation, for instance.

The aviation editor for the UPI, Robert Buckhorn, quoted this bit of industry obfuscation: "The cause of the crash was the pilot's failure to maintain sufficient altitude to avoid neighboring terrain."

Meaning: "The plane flew into the side of a hill."

Here's another way to describe a crash in gobbledygook: "The pilot's apparently unrecognized descent to an altitude below that of the airport." In the inner world of aviation, engines never "fall off;" they "detach themselves." Airplanes don't "crash;" they make "uncontrolled descents into the ground."

MORE FOG TO FLOG

One shouldn't place all the blame for gobbledygook on lower-level bureaucrats. A recent President who was fond of introducing remarks by saying: "I want to make it perfectly clear . . ." also said this: "The rise in the rate of increase is downward rather than upward." He was talking about the economy . . . I think.

A newspaper story included this quote: " 'Wallace has communicated with me to say he is sending a letter that he plans to run here as a Democrat,' Massachusetts Secretary of State John F. X. Davoren said."

Politicians do talk like that, don't they? Twenty-one words to say this: "Wallace told me that he plans to run here as a Democrat." Just 12 words get the message across more effectively. One shudders at the thought of the thousands of trees which have been murdered to make paper on which politicians and bureaucrats have maundered and meandered down the years.

And educators, too. Here's another newspaper quote:

> **"In an attempt to clarify a statement made regarding a new tax base, Napoleon County School Superintendent Tim V. Klocker said today there would be little or no difference in the amount of property taxes paid with a new tax base.**
>
> **" 'The tax presently levied to raise money for the present tax base, plus the amount in excess of it, would equal the taxes that would be levied for the new tax base,' Klocker explained."**

He did?

Words can be used as smokescreens by timid souls who don't intend to be pinned down. Consider this example from a government letter: "It would probably be possible to make an affirmative finding, subject to the usual requirements normally established for situations seemingly of this general type."

Isn't that breathtaking? It says nothing the first time you read it and it says less with each successive reading. The person who wrote that is certain to go far in government.

INTERNATIONAL SMOG

Verbal smog is by no means an exclusively American phenomenon. This sentence was written to a superior by the manager of a branch post office in England: "Verbal contact with Mr. Blank regarding the attached notification of promotion has elicited the attached representation intimating that he prefers to decline the assignment."

A writing handbook said this should have been slashed, to wit: "I have spoken to Mr. Blank about this promotion; he does not wish to accept the post offered."

A newspaperman went further: "Blank doesn't want the job."

The 24 words of the first sentence have been shrunk to five; all the necessary information remains and the short sentence cannot be misunderstood. You might call it "creative cutting."

George Orwell, the renowned English writer, suggested that if the government had written the Biblical passage: "The race is not to the swift, nor the battle to the strong . . .," it would have come out as: "Objective consideration of contemporary phenomena compels the conclusion that success or failure in competitive activities exhibits no tendency to be commensurate with innate capacity."

We mustn't get surly about this, though. Gobbledygook can be fun. The game consists of translating the following gobbledygook proverbs into English, preferably without peeking at the translations. Anyone who gets a perfect score without using a dictionary may choose between two prizes: a lifetime job with the U.S. Department of Agriculture (Sheep Dip Division), or a fur-lined model of the Pentagon, complete with dancing admirals.

PROVERBS

1. **It is unwise to scrutinize the masticating apparatus of a donated equine.**
2. **That which appeals to a flesh-eater may seem toxic to another.**
3. **Toil is rendered trifling by application of a large aggregation.**
4. **The completion of incubation should take place prior to the census enumeration of one's fowl.**
5. **An aged canine cannot be educated to innovative attainment.**
6. **A single hirundine bird does not indicate the estival season.**
7. **The want of aquatic liquid is not apparent prior to the depletion of the bore.**
8. **Two quarter-portions of the staff of life exceed in value the lack of any.**
9. **The exercise of choice is denied the mendicant.**
10. **Those who inhabit dwellings of a brittle transparent substance should refrain from the propulsion of geological specimens.**

11. The pilferer may best be apprehended by another of the same persuasion.
12. An overabundance of culinary practitioners bungles the preparation of a liquid food.

TRANSLATIONS

1. Don't look a gift horse in the mouth.
2. One man's meat is another man's poison.
3. Many hands make light work.
4. Don't count your chickens before they're hatched.
5. You can't teach an old dog new tricks.
6. One swallow does not make a summer.
7. You never miss the water 'til the well runs dry.
8. Half a loaf is better than none.
9. Beggars can't be choosers.
10. People who live in glass houses shouldn't throw stones.
11. Set a thief to catch a thief.
12. Too many cooks spoil the soup.

There is no end to fun and games with gobbledygook. Consider this government memo: "All officers wishing to take advantage of the girls in the secretarial pool should call Ext. 81." And this progress report on a typist: "She is willing to struggle if given the opportunity."

WORD PLAY

In his column, "The Once Over," H. I. Phillips once had a giggle over gobbledygook. I quote:

"A DIRECTIVE"

"It all began with the following:

Little Boy Blue, come blow your horn:
The cows are in the meadow,
The sheep are in the corn;
Where's the boy who looks after the sheep?
He is under the haystack fast asleep.

"Ultimately a Washington Bureaucrat took over:

"In accordance with the act of Congress of June 6, 1923, as amended, we have conducted an extensive inquiry into the need for an adequate signal system in meadows and adjacent territories. The whole matter of stabilizing practices in these areas is being processed with a view to attaining the objectives as stated in the directive of July 7. Considering the matter in the overall aspect, it is the conclusion of our policy committee, following repeated hearings, that the following steps are necessary to restore confidence and maintain morale:

"1. Immediate stimulation of the entire horn-blowing project.

"2. A study to determine standards with reference to the proper number of blasts to be blown when cows are in the meadow.

"3. A signal system requiring a signal easily distinguishable from the former when the sheep are reported in the corn.

"4. Authorization for a complete study of the whole farm situation, and a check-up of the bugle crisis, with possible freezing of bugle calls at April levels in accordance with the so-called Little Haystack Formula.

"5. A congressional inquiry to ascertain the number of meadows in the country, the square miles of corn patches and the wandering habits of sheep and cattle.

"6. A census to determine how many boys in the country are under a mandate to look after sheep.

"7. A study to determine whether these boys are subject to abnormal indolence or excessive slumber.

"8. An appropriation of five million dollars to provide adequate handling of the haystack matter, to assure an adequate distribution of horns and to take all necessary steps to integrate, codify and coordinate all authorized operation.

"For the purpose of keeping our files accurate, will you inform us of your correct name? It appears on our records as L. Boice Blow, Little B. Bloo and L. Iittle Boybluh.

"U.S. COW, SHEEP AND HAYSTACK ADMINISTRATION, Washington, D.C."

You get the idea. If gobbledygook is a disease, there seems to be a lot of it around. So stay out of drafts, keep your brain warm and dry and remember that immortal bumper sticker: "Eschew Obfuscation."

SOMETHING TO READ

I know you'll be pleased to hear that gobbledygook can be reduced to a formula. Philip Broughton of the U.S. Public Health Service hit upon the method, which he calls the "Systematic Phrase Projector." Broughton uses 30 carefully chosen "buzzwords," and here they are:

Column A	*Column B*	*Column C*
0. integrated	0. management	0. options
1. total	1. organizational	1. flexibility
2. systematized	2. monitored	2. capability
3. parallel	3. reciprocal	3. mobility
4. functional	4. digital	4. programming
5. responsive	5. logistical	5. concept
6. optional	6. transitional	6. time-phase
7. synchronized	7. incremental	7. projection
8. compatible	8. third-generation	8. distention
9. balanced	9. policy	9. contingency

To use Broughton's system for Instant Gobbledygook, you have only to think of a three-digit number, like "492." From Broughton's buzzword list, pick one from Column A, one from Column B and one from Column C. The number "492" becomes "functional policy capability."

Wow! At least a million dollars of government spending could be justified with a phrase like that.

Said Broughton: "No one will have the remotest idea of what you are talking about but the important thing is that they're not about to admit it."

Which is the secret of gobbledygook, right?

SOMETHING TO WRITE

Write a communique from the U.S. Department of Defense to the Senate Foreign Relations Committee, with a Broughton buzzword content of at least 40 per cent. The communique justifies a war on Tierra del Fuego.

First, though, check your sex and military draft status.

SOMETHING MORE TO WRITE

A government agency sent a letter containing the following paragraph to more than 100,000 persons over a period of seven years:

> **"In order to be fully insured, an individual must have earned $50 or more in covered employment for as many quarters of coverage as half the calendar quarters elapsing between 1935 and the quarter in which he reaches 65 or dies, whichever first occurs."**

First, decipher that clot of words, if you can. Then rewrite it so that it makes sense to the average taxpayer. Lots of luck . . .

SOMETHING TO THINK ABOUT

"Words are like leaves; and where they most abound, much fruit of sense is rarely found."

—Alexander Pope

"I am convinced more and more day by day that fine writing is, next to fine doing, the top thing in the world."

—John Keats

9. Tricks of the Trade

Some professional writers analyze what they do and how they do it; others just do it.

I've always been the analytical type, possibly because analyzing is less fatiguing than writing. Like Mark Twain, I have never considered fatigue to be an especially desirable condition of mind and body. As a result, I devote vast amounts of conniving time to making writing easier. Or at least *possible*.

I noticed during my teaching years that many students take the same approach. If all the energy spent in thinking and talking about writing (and how to postpone writing) could have been devoted to actually writing, the world would now be splitting apart under a load of printed pages.

So those of use who analyze, who try to make this writing job easier, are performing a public service, if you want to look at it that way. Let's look at it that way, since we have a towering figure like Mark Twain on our side.

The title of this chapter, as you may have noticed, is "Tricks of the Trade." This might as well have been the title for the book. The book could also have been called: "Hard Work Made Slightly Easier." If the world's lazy persons get no credit for anything else, they should be rewarded for practically inventing efficiency.

THOSE EYES AT MY ELBOW

It is dangerous for any writer to assume that a reader is going to be very interested in what he has to say. Generally it is safer to assume that your reader is going to be slightly bored by what you have to say, at least at the beginning, and if you want to communicate, you must deliver in a way that kindles his interest, stings him and finally impales him on your lance.

A student has a special problem in this regard because usually the student is writing for a teacher. And nearly always, when the teacher is reading, he or she is reading the top paper from a tall stack. After several hours of burrowing through tedious pap, any teacher can be forgiven for losing interest in reading.

The student, then, faces a formidable task: rekindling a fire in the cold ashes of a teacher's brain.

When students have a choice of subject matter for a writing assignment, they should always choose a subject that interests them, not one that is merely convenient and easily researched. Chances are excellent that this interest will glow through the finished writing.

But it is not enough that the subject interest the writer; it must also interest the reader. The writer who loses sight of his reader is not really writing at all; he is merely making marks on paper.

By nature, writing is a lonely job. But if writers let their loneliness delude them into thinking that there is no one out there, they make a disastrous mistake. There is always an invisible audience at a writer's elbow; the audience is composed of readers. The good writer is always conscious of all those eyes at his elbow.

Not that there is anything wrong with writing as mental therapy. A writer spilling his hangups onto paper is better off than if he were out burning down buildings . . . and so is society. But these writers aren't communicating; they are just contemplating their navels.

The writer who wants to be read can't afford very much self-indulgence. Readers are busy; readers are demanding. Readers don't want to pat a writer's fevered hand; they want their own hands patted, fevered or not.

Without readers, writers are nothing. So pat a few hands and score a few points.

CARE AND FEEDING OF THE BRAIN

Brains, like muscles, get tired. Tired brains limp, too.

You mustn't demand more of your brain than it can deliver. Few writers can put in more than three or four consecutive hours of concentrated work, certainly not as a daily routine. Writing demands the best that your brain can produce. Once tired, your brain may be capable of typing, but not of writing.

Quit; rest; start the fountain flowing another day after the reservoir has refilled.

For most persons, writing is a slow process. The mind can create images rapidly but they often appear on paper slowly. Some images flit across the mind so quickly that they cannot be grasped and impaled on paper; they may then be lost forever. This is why it is better to learn to type rapidly and then write at the typewriter than to laboriously scrawl with a pen. It's like swatting flies; you score better with a swatter than with a bare hand. Fewer flies and fewer images get away.

Typing helps in another way, too. A teacher who has read 40 consecutive hand-scrawled themes is likely to emit glad little squeals when a typed one turns up. Learning to type isn't terribly difficult; you don't even have to enroll in a typing class. All you need to know, at bottom, is which fingers to put where; the rest is merely practice. And more practice. Borrow a typing manual, get the fingers figured out, then have at it.

You will have to become fairly proficient as a typist before you can actually write at the typewriter. At first, you'll be thinking about what your fingers are doing instead of what your brain is doing. In time, you won't even be conscious of your fingers or the machine, but only of those precious words spreading across the paper at the rate of 40 or 50 per minute . . . on a good day.

Truth is, handwriting is rapidly becoming obsolete and the day is near when pens will be used mostly for signing checks. Why not make every week "Be kind to English Teachers Week?" Type those compositions and eventually learn to compose at the typewriter. Do it and you'll find that you are grabbing more of those thoughts and images before they slide off into the mist from which they came.

TELEPHONES AND OTHER WRONG NUMBERS

American author Henry Miller has said: "I'd rather sit down and write a brief note than call someone up. I hate telephones. I owe my beginnings as a writer to the fact that long ago when I worked in my father's tailor shop, I had lots of spare time and I wrote letters, letters galore. Long letters—20, 30, 40 pages. To friends. These letters were talking about the books I'd just read, or the museums I went to, or they were explorations. Letter writing, I think, gave me my natural style."

Most persons find letter writing difficult. Of course; writing is writing. But letter writing is writing practice and there is no substitute for practice, whether you want to learn to write or to walk on water.

For some writers, it is helpful to revise a piece of writing many times, each time with a specific purpose in mind. This can be more productive than trying to catch everything on one trip through. You might check your manuscripts once for grammar and spelling, then for paragraphing, then for factual accuracy, then for excess wordage.

When the words begin to blur or sound silly, it's time to stop. It is possible to revise a piece of writing so much that it goes dead. You are tired of it; it's that simple. Once you reach this stale point, continued revision may do more harm than good. Put the thing away for a day or two, dislodge it from the front of your mind and you may find when you get back to it that it seems fresh again.

Many students are confused about the comparative difficulty of writing something long or short. Accustomed to writing 250-word papers, they groan passionately when a teacher assigns a 500-word paper.

The truth is, if you're going about it right, it is easier to write about something that interests you in 500 words than in 250. If you are going about it wrong, perhaps writing about something which doesn't interest you, writing a 50-word paper is terribly difficult. You can't roll a square boulder uphill.

ALL THOSE WORDS!

Dictionaries can be very useful to a writer, but also very

frightening. All those words! Is a writer supposed to know all of them? Or even one-tenth of them?

Of course not. A dictionary is like a smorgasbord; if you have half a brain, you don't stuff yourself to the point of explosion after entering either. All those words are there for the same reason all that food is there—so you can pick and choose.

Having discovered all those words in that great big book, a student's first serious brush with humility may come when he discovers that putting them in the right order can be a bit of a trick. Some students think that a dictionary ought to be kept at their elbow as they write. Not necessarily; stumped for a word, you might do better to leave a blank and rush on. If you interrupt the flow of words onto paper, you might have difficulty starting it again.

A better idea: use a dictionary only during revision. You can afford to wait; I can promise you that all the right words will still be there, frozen on those pages.

To professional writers, a dictionary is useful mostly as a spelling aid. You may be surprised to hear that professional authors have to cope with spelling problems, too, but it's true; some are good spellers, others are atrocious. But the bad spellers are too smart to let themselves be caught in the act by editors or readers. Why should they, when all the words are spelled correctly in the dictionary?

Spelling is largely witchcraft. No one is quite sure why one person is a good speller and another, just as intelligent, is a poor one. I used to expound a theory that the only way to learn spelling was to read widely. It seemed to me that anyone who sees a word spelled correctly often enough soon will learn how to spell that word. After all, I think that's how I learned to spell.

My theory began to develop embarrassing holes as I encountered more and more persons who read widely and still couldn't spell for sour apples. If you happen to be one of these individuals, why worry? Just keep a good dictionary at your elbow. You don't have to be a good speller so long as that blessed book is.

Since I've never had a spelling problem, I consider another kind of word book more useful than a dictionary. I refer to a thesaurus. If you have used the verb "run" too often in a paragraph and want an interesting substitute, the dictionary probably won't help you much. A thesaurus will; instead of giving definitions, it provides words with the same meaning, or almost the same meaning. If, during revision, you smell a dead word in your opening paragraph, you can usually find a living, breathing substitute in a thesaurus.

SAYING WHAT WAS SAID

Playwrights, probably, were the first to write dialogue. Then fiction writers took it up as a means of making characters come alive. Human beings *do* tend to talk a lot. When we write about human beings and try to make them seem real, it makes sense to have them talk. That is, to come right out and blurt:

"Take your hands off me, you foul fiend!"

This is better than solemnly proclaiming that the heroine objected to her treatment at the hands of the bearded ruffian. Much better . . .

So fiction writers created talking characters. Recognizing a good thing, newspaper writers picked up the trick. Writers of non-fiction books weren't far behind.

Possibly running a good thing into the ground, some modern writers have created books, both non-fiction and fiction, which consist mostly of dialogue. Students of writing ought to be aware of this trend.

Writing good dialogue isn't easy. It isn't just a matter of recording real talk on paper; most real talk is disjointed, repetitive, fragmented and sometimes barely comprehensible when recorded on tape. Good written dialogue is what real talk ought to be, but seldom is.

There is only one way to learn how to write good, real-sounding dialogue: Write lots of it, then read it back aloud. If it sounds silly, it may be truly realistic dialogue. Rewrite it; you want something better.

Let's say that you have principles and are trying to live with them. You don't want to quote somebody directly in your writing because you don't remember exactly what was said; you remember only the gist of what was said and somehow it doesn't seem entirely honest to put the gist in direct quotes.

Well, if it isn't, every American newspaper is dishonest and has been for at least 50 years. Most newspaper quotes contained in official-looking quotation marks are only an approximation of what the quoted individual actually said. If newspapers quoted all of their sources exactly, they would go bankrupt from lawsuits.

In modern factual writing, a direct quotation is *approximately* what was said by the person quoted. The excess wordage has been taken out; the profanity has been taken out; the libel has been taken out.

A student writer would be wise to practice dialogue writing and wiser still to use dialogue in his writing, even if it isn't very good dialogue at first. Modern writing almost *demands* it.

"This is all I have to say about dialogue," he said, covering his typewriter.

A man who is considered by some (like me) to be the finest writer America has produced, Mark Twain, once wrote to a young friend:

> **"I notice that you use plain, simple language, short words and brief sentences. This is the way to write English. It is the modern way and the best way. Stick to it."**

Of course, being Mark Twain, a supremely funny man

who also intended to become a rich one, he said the same thing in another way:

> **"I never write 'metropolis' for seven cents when I can get the same price for 'city.' "**

There was a time in this country's history when a city slicker using big words could bamboozle his country cousins. Now a city slicker trying that trick is likely to get slugged with an unabridged dictionary.

FOG FINALLY FLOGGED!

The best book about writing that I know of is *The Technique of Clear Writing,* by Robert Gunning. For many years, Gunning has worked as a writing consultant for business and government.

One of Gunning's major tools is a formula called the "Fog Index." By applying this formula, anyone can quickly evaluate a piece of writing for its fog content. The result is expressed in a number that corresponds roughly to school grade reading level. The formula is concerned primarily with two measurements: word length and sentence length.

This is how you find the Fog Index:

> **"One: Jot down the number of words in successive sentences. If the piece is long, you may wish to take several samples of 100 words, spaced evenly through it. If you do, stop the sentence count with the sentence which ends nearest the 100-word total. Divide the total number of words in the passage by the number of sentences. This gives the average sentence length of the passage.**
>
> **"Two. Count the number of words of three syllables or more per 100 words. Don't count the words (1) that are proper names, (2) that are combinations of short easy words (like 'bookkeeper' and 'manpower'), (3) that are verb forms made three syllables by adding *-ed* or *es* (like 'created' or 'trespasses'). This gives you the percentage of hard words in the passage.**

"Three: To get the Fog Index, total the two factors just counted and multiply by .4."

And that's all there is to it. A person who hasn't forgotten simple arithmetic can apply the formula in a few minutes.

Gunning cautions that his formula is not meant to be used as a pattern *while* you write but as a yardstick *after* you've written. He points out, too, that the formula is not entirely a mechanical process; some judgment must be applied. There are words of three or more syllables which are not difficult at all—words like "newspaper" or "battleship." (On the other hand, one can compose a paragraph of rare one-syllable words which would have a very low Fog Index while remaining completely incomprehensible to a college graduate.) Also, Gunning recommends that two complete thoughts linked by a semi-colon be counted as two sentences, not one.

Gunning sets the danger line at a Fog Index of 13. Beyond this point, you run the risk of reader fatigue, and your message may go a-glimmering because you tried so hard to think like a writer that you forgot to think like a reader.

Reader's Digest is read by 17 million persons, which makes it the mass circulation magazine to end all. To achieve such enormous readership, the magazine must be intelligible and interesting to persons at many age and education levels. Where would you expect its Fog Index to fall?

Gunning puts it at 10. News magazines such as *Time* are one point higher. "Class" magazines, such as *Harper's* and *Atlantic Monthly,* reach their select, well-educated readership with a Fog Index of 12.

OUT OF THE MURK

Gunning once was asked by a client to check the readability of Thomas Paine, who happened to be one of the client's favorite writers. Gunning found that this revolutionary leader's prose tested above the danger line. But he also discovered that the parts of Paine's writing for which he is most famous tested well below the danger line, like the following paragraph:

> "These are the times that try men's souls: The summer soldier and the sunshine patriot will in this crisis, shrink from the service of his country; but he that stands it now, deserves the love and thanks of man and woman. Tyranny, like hell, is not easily conquered; yet we have this consolation with us, that the harder the conflict, the more glorious the triumph. What we obtain too cheap, we esteem too lightly;—'Tis dearness only that gives everything its value. Heaven knows how to put a proper price upon its goods; and it would be strange indeed, if so celestial an article as freedom should not be highly rated."

According to Gunning, the Fog Index of that historic paragraph is only 7. Immortal writing is usually simple writing.

Gunning makes an interesting point about short vs. long words. We need long words, he writes, to *think* with, but when we try to pass along our thoughts to others, we must translate into short words. Sometimes, of course, the long word is the only *right* word, in which case proper meaning takes precedence. A correct long word is always better than an incorrect short word.

Many widely-read authors — John Steinbeck, for example, to mention another of my heroes—have Fog Indexes in the 8-10 range. Any student writer who exceeds this level probably ought to go soak his head, then try again.

The quickest way to reduce Fog Index is by cutting average length of sentences. The key word is "average." (*Reader's Digest* average sentence length is between 14 and 17.) Sentence variety is tremendously important in putting rhythm into writing. A piece of writing with all its sentences in the 14-17 range would have an unpleasant sing-song effect. Some should be short, some should be long and some should be in-between. Deciding which should be which is the writer's job; no formula can help.

If average sentence length is reduced, but the Fog Index remains too high, there is only one more place to look for trouble; long and difficult words. Root them out; you have nothing to lose but your fog and you have a priceless reward to gain: the attention of your readers. Airplanes have radar to help them find their way through fog; too often, writers write as if readers were similarly equipped.

WHO NEEDS A SKELETON?

Some teachers of writing (and students, too) are much concerned about outlines. Thinking of outlines as road maps, they ask: "How can you get where you're going if you don't know where 'where' is?"

Makes sense. It is better to outline than to flounder around. But . . .

It is possible to put so much creative energy into an outline that there is little left for writing. *Tell your story once* . . . remember?

Some professional writers outline very carefully. Others don't. The rule for you is the rule that works for you.

A FINAL TINY TRICK

Punch lines always come last. I know that; you know that; everybody knows that. Yet, it's surprisingly easy to forget that simple little gimmick.

A friend of mine wrote an excellent magazine article in which a father went for a ride in a son's car. An accident occurred. When the dust had settled, the son asked, "Are you hurt, Dad? Want to go to a doctor?"

"No," the father replied. "Since only a jackass would ride in this contraption, better take me to a veterinarian."

Not bad; the point is made. But look at what happens if you switch that last line like this:

"No," the father replied. "Better take me to a veterinarian. Only a jackass would ride in this contraption."

Isn't that sharper? A small thing, but what is writing but one small thing after another?

SOMETHING TO WRITE

Figure the Fog Index of your last piece of writing, then analyze the result in 300 words or less. Then figure the Fog Index of your analysis and explain the discrepancy. When you have recovered from that, figure the Fog Index of this book and if it's more than 8, write me a nasty letter.

SOMETHING TO GLOAT ABOUT

It has been said that if 10,000 high school graduates write from dictation the sentence which follows, at least 9999 of them will misspell at least one word:

"Outside a cemetery stood a harassed beggar and an embarrassed peddler gauging the symmetry of a lady's ankle with unparalleled ecstasy."

You might try that sentence on a few of those parents who insist that kids aren't learning to spell these days.

SOMETHING TO THINK ABOUT

> *"Contrary to what most students want and expect, a teacher is not a bridegroom: he can open the door to truth, but he cannot carry you across the threshold and deposit you safely on the other side."*
>
> —Sydney J. Harris

"It gives me great delight to hear that you have learned to sit still, and read a book. If you have really accomplished that, you have certainly made your fortune."
—Sen. Daniel Webster
in a letter to his son, 1836

10. The Loose End

One of the most pleasant aspects of being a writer is that you inevitably get to know other writers and they are inclined to be interesting people who write long, fascinating letters.

Once in a while, too, they ask for criticism of something they've written. So you agonize a little. Do they really want criticism? Or do they want praise? Do you want to give them what they want? Or do you want to tell them the truth?

A student writer often has the same problem. Somebody says: "Hey, ol' buddy, would you read this and tell me what's wrong with it? If I don't get at least a 'B' on this one, I'm dead."

Hoping that the stuff is really good, you take the paper, read it, and conclude that your ol' buddy is dead. It's a C-minus, or worse, and it's time again for a Hard Choice.

If you are running for Alfalfa Queen or Head Honcho, you really ought to tell ol' buddy that this piece of writing is probably the greatest thing since Shakespeare turned in his quill.

But if you have no political ambitions, and have more friends than you can use anyway, you ought to tell ol' buddy that his baby needs a complete change of diapers or he's down the tube in English. Do you want to be popular? Or honest? Sometimes you have to choose.

Unfortunately, most of the non-professionals who pass along their writing want praise, not criticism. This is true even when they ask for criticism. Only a very strong, well-balanced personality can coolly accept (and put to good use) criticism of those glowing words just torn from his warm brain and engraved upon paper.

When my writer friends ask me for criticism (and once in a while when they don't), I give it with as much honesty as I can muster at the moment. Then I brace myself, thinking: *Scratch one friend.* It seems to work, after a fashion; I still have a few friends. That is, prior to the publication of this book . . .

READING IS WRITING: WRITING IS READNG

Did it ever occur to you that just about anything you want to know—*anything at all*—is available somewhere on a printed page? All you have to do is find the right book or magazine or newspaper; then the whole world's wisdom and knowledge and experience are at your fingertips.

Before you can write well, you must *read* and *read* and

read, until you read easily and well, until you read without even thinking about the act of reading, until you read out of unbreakable habit every printed word that passes before your eyes, down to and including the stunning messages on the jars and boxes which litter the breakfast table.

Reading is to writing what inhaling is to exhaling. They're not the same but they are part of the same process; one must precede the other and co-exist with the other. Reading can do more than almost anything else to help your writing. *Almost* anything else. Finally, to learn to write, you will have to write and write some more, then do some more writing.

Okay, you say, reading is great but what about personal experience? Isn't it better to have actually experienced what you write about?

Maybe, but life is short and for most of us, rather restricted. Also, unless the rules have been changed in my absence, we are allowed only one life per customer. A reader can live many lives, if only vicariously. He needn't be limited in his writing to those experiences squeezed from real life.

A writer can acquire information in many ways. He can operate like a newspaper reporter, investigating on the spot and interviewing. This is usually the most enjoyable research, because it involves adventure, but it isn't always possible. Reading remains the quickest, most efficient method.

Once I wrote a novel with an aviation background. My brother, a private pilot, read the book and expressed surprise at my apparent knowledge of flying. He was not aware that I had spent so much time hanging around airports and flying airplanes.

I hadn't. I had visited airports frequently but seldom for more than an hour at a time. I had flown an airplane for a total of five minutes; as a passenger, I had endured one loop in a plane not designed for looping; I almost threw up. Most of my information had come from reading. I had acquired what I call a "writer's knowledge" of the subject. In other words, I knew enough to be able to make my writing sound as if I knew a great deal more.

Does that sound dishonest? If it is, most writers are dishonest, because they offer not reality, but the *appearance* of reality. This is the essence of the writer's art. Most writers reach a point, reluctantly, where they must stop researching and start writing, well aware that there are enormous gaps in their knowledge. Often a student must do the same, without guilt, without qualms.

The key tool is *reading,* which can turn you into an apparent expert on almost anything, with surprising speed.

Dr. George Gallup, the poll-taking man, told a convention of newspaper publishers: "Unless an individual spends at least one hour and 45 minutes a day reading newspapers, magazines, books, he is not going very far."

Results of his organization's studies indicated that students who spend the most time reading are usually those who lead their classes. Also, students who spend most of their leisure time watching television are most likely to become dropouts. It figures . . .

In the old days, American society was agrarian; most of us lived and worked on farms, or lived in small towns and worked on surrounding farms. Then, less than a century ago, along came something called the Industrial Revolution, offering work and wages and high life in the cities; we gladly left the farms for the factories.

Now, some experts say, we have passed through the industrial age and entered something called the "information society," in which only those who can absorb information at a rapid rate can compete successfully. No one has yet invented a more rapid way of absorbing information than reading. The lesson is clear: READ. This is how you make it in school and out of school.

On the other hand, there's a terrific show on Channel 2. Put down the book, slump on your neck and watch it. It will give you something to talk about in the unemployment line.

READING IS NICE: WRITING IS NICER

Reading is input but writing is output. It is output which finally determines success in education. Perhaps I feel strongly about the importance of writing because of an experience I had in education. Once, in a fit of energy, I earned an undergraduate degree in journalism. Then, for five years, I wrote words for newspapers, thousands of words each working day, millions of words each working year, most of the words under deadline pressure.

Then I went back to college in search of a graduate degree, fearing that the long layoff would make me sweat for it.

Surprise! It was easy. Reports, term papers and essay examinations flowed out of my typewriter like honey from a hive and my grades were great. I had never before done so well in school.

Moral: Teachers are impressed by students who read; they are *dazzled* by students who write.

THE FINAL FACE-UP

You can read all the books that have ever been written about writing and listen to lectures about writing until your ears twang but when you finally face the blank, accusing sheet of paper, you must realize that your writing is YOU . . . and you're stuck with you.

If your writing is to improve, only YOU can improve it, with, perhaps, a little help from your friends. Teachers and books like this one can give you an occasional nudge in the right direction but that's all. According to rumor, God can make a tree, but He can't make a writer out of you. Only you can do that.

Right there is writing's greatest challenge and, when

the job is done, writing's greatest satisfaction.

The student who writes a theme for a grade is doing the same thing as the professional author who writes a book for a buck. The motivation is the same: self-advancement. The ingredients are the same: words. The tool is the same: technique.

The differences are only a matter of degree. If the student doesn't write well, he gets an "F." If the professional doesn't write well, he starves. The professional does more and better work because he has several advantages:

(1) Avoiding starvation is stronger motivation than avoiding a bad grade.

(2) The professional has lived longer than the student and as a result, he has read more words . . . millions more.

(3) By writing and writing and writing, the professional has honed his technique.

Long ago, the professional faced up to the fact that there is only one way to learn writing—by writing. Students should face up to it, too.

Sorry about that. I never promised you a rose garden.

FOR TEACHERS AND OVER-ACHIEVING STUDENTS . . . MORE BOOKS ABOUT WRITING

Gunning, Robert; *The Technique of Clear Writing;* McGraw-Hill; 1968 (Revised edition).

In my opinion, this is the best general book ever written about writing. Gunning is a professional writing consultant and one of few writers-about-writing who applies his principles in his own published work. Anyone with writing notions should have this book in his personal library and should re-read it once a year.

O'Hayre, John; *Gobbledygook Has Gotta Go;* U.S. Government Printing Office.

At a price of 40 cents, this has to be the best bargain around. In a light, bright presentation, O'Hayre snaps at federal government writers to good effect but his preachments have a much wider application.

Linton, Calvin D.; *Effective Revenue Writing 2;* Training Manual No. 129; U.S. Government Printing Office.

You'll never see that title on a movie marquee but a book shouldn't be judged by its cover . . . nor by its title. Like O'Hayre's book, this lively effort is aimed at federal government writers but the message is valid wherever writers write.

Strunk, William, Jr. and White, E. B.; *The Elements of Style;* The Macmillan Company.

This book is almost a cliche, has sold a ridiculous number of copies and has been issued recently in a new edition. It's just a little book, easily portable, and especially strong in mechanical aspects of writing. It's also a bit musty in an Ivy League sort of way, but it's useful just the same.

Payne, Lucile Vaughan; *The Lively Art of Writing;* Follett Educational Corporation.

This book was recommended highly by a former English teacher whose opinion I respect. Its concept is narrow in that it concentrates on the essay form but this approach is probably relevant since students usually are assigned to write essays of sorts. The book includes a depressing amount of end-of-chapter busy work. I suppose some teachers will appreciate this even if students won't. My friend, the former English teacher, said that many of her students wrote letters to the author in praise of the book, a good sign. (As a textbook author, I know how rare such a reaction is.) Quibbling aside, this is a crisp, no-nonsense book which bears the clear imprint of a professional author and teacher.

SELECTED BIBLIOGRAPHY

Crist, Lyle M.; *Man Expressed: The Realm of Writing;* Macmillan; 1971.

Hall, Milton; *Getting Your Ideas Across Through Writing;* U.S. Government Printing Office; 1970.

Hall, Lawrence Sargent; *How Thinking Is Written;* D. C. Heath & Co.; 1963.

Lambuth, David, and others; *The Golden Book on Writing;* The Viking Press; 1964.

Linday, Catherine; *How to Teach Your Students to Write;* Funk & Wagnalls; 1967.

Riemer, George; *How They Murdered the Second R;* Creative Writing Service, 149 Clinton St., Brooklyn Heights, N.Y.; 1969.

Vrooman, Alan H.; *Good Writing: An Informal Manual of Style;* The Phillips Exeter Academy Press-Atheneum; 1967.

OLSON'S COMMANDMENTS
(I through X)

I—Find a private place in which to write and guard it with your life; words abhor crowds.

II—Write regularly; don't wait for the crack of the whip.

III—Tell your story only once . . . and tell it on paper.

IV—When writing a first draft, don't let yourself get bogged down in picky details.

V—Whenever possible, write about subjects which truly interest you; bored writers produce bored readers.

VI—Revise for specific purposes.

VII—Never use two long words when a short one will do.

VIII—Use rules as yardsticks, not as crutches.

IX—Remember that getting started is half the battle.

X—Remember that getting started is half the battle.

OLSON'S COMMANDMENTS
(I through X)

I—Find a private place in which to write and guard it with your life; words abhor crowds.

II—Write regularly; don't wait for the crack of the whip.

III—Tell your story only once . . . and tell it on paper.

IV—When writing a first draft, don't let yourself get bogged down in picky details.

V—Whenever possible, write about subjects which truly interest you; bored writers produce bored readers.

VI—Revise for specific purposes.

VII—Never use two long words when a short one will do.

VIII—Use rules as yardsticks, not as crutches.

IX—Remember that getting started is half the battle.

X—Remember that getting started is half the battle.

OLSON'S COMMANDMENTS
(I through X)

I—Find a private place in which to write and guard it with your life; words abhor crowds.

II—Write regularly; don't wait for the crack of the whip.

III—Tell your story only once . . . and tell it on paper.

IV—When writing a first draft, don't let yourself get bogged down in picky details.

V—Whenever possible, write about subjects which truly interest you; bored writers produce bored readers.

VI—Revise for specific purposes.

VII—Never use two long words when a short one will do.

VIII—Use rules as yardsticks, not as crutches.

IX—Remember that getting started is half the battle.

X—Remember that getting started is half the battle.

GENE OL[illegible] career to be able to write about writing. *Sweet Ago*[illegible] published book in a professional writing car[illegible] back to 1945. His output includes both fictio[illegible] and nonfiction. He has written many books for teenage[illegible] and a few for adults and [illegible] for plain peop[illegible] wholly accepted the generation gap.)

HE HAS ALSO WRITTEN for daily and weekly newspapers, for magazines and for television. He sold the first short story he wrote and the first novel. At intervals along the way, he taught high school English in Camarillo, California, and Portland, Oregon. In *Sweet Agony* he has tried to distill in a tightly-written book the pure residue of his experience in writing and teaching.

OLSON'S INTENT in *Sweet Agony* is not to help student writers become professionals; he wants only to pass along those parts of professional experience which can lead students toward a better understanding of the writing process and help them to cope more cheerfully with its enormous difficulties. And, not incidentally, he would like to make the job of [illegible] more productive and satisfying by making it less baffling.

OLSON SAYS: "Writing is hard work. Teaching writing is at least as hard. Writers and teachers of writing need all the help they can get. I think it's time we started helping each other."

That's what *Sweet Agony* is all about.